THE GREAT LIVES SERIES

Great Lives biographies shed an exciting new light on the many dynamic men and women whose actions, visions, and dedication to an ideal have influenced the course of history. Their ambitions, dreams, successes, and failures, the controversies they faced and the obstacles they overcame are the true stories behind these distinguished world leaders, explorers, and great Americans.

Other biographies in the Great Lives Series

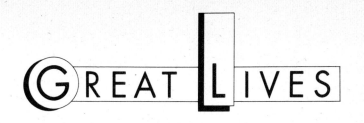

FRANKLIN D. ROOSEVELT
THE PEOPLE'S PRESIDENT

By John D. Selfridge

FAWCETT COLUMBINE
NEW YORK

For middle-school readers

A Fawcett Columbine Book
Published by Ballantine Books

Produced by
The Jeffrey Weiss Group, Inc.
96 Morton Street
New York, New York 10014

Library of Congress Catalog Card Number: 89-90908

ISBN: 0-449-90401-6

Cover design and illustration by Paul Davis

Manufactured in the United States of America

First Edition: February 1990

10 9 8 7 6 5 4 3 2 1

ACKNOWLEDGMENT

A special thanks to educators Dr. Frank Moretti, Ph.D., Associate Headmaster of the Dalton School in New York City; Dr. Paul Mattingly, Ph.D., Professor of History at New York University; and Barbara Smith, M.S., Assistant Superintendent of the Los Angeles Unified School District, for their contributions to the Great Lives Series.

FRANKLIN D. ROOSEVELT
THE PEOPLE'S PRESIDENT

TABLE OF CONTENTS

President Franklin Delano Roosevelt during a live radio broadcast of one of his famous "fireside chats" in 1937. Roosevelt believed in explaining directly to the American public what was happening with their government. In doing so on a regular basis he forged a bond with the people that few presidents since have been able to match.

1

Pearl Harbor

U.S. president Franklin Delano Roosevelt hit the campaign trail in 1940 seeking reelection to a third term. That fall, in Cleveland, Ohio, he delivered a speech that many consider the most eloquent of his political career. Looking out at his audience and speaking in his usual, resonating tone, he asked for their support: "There is a storm raging now, a storm that makes things harder for the world. And that storm, which did not start in this land of ours, is the true reason that I would like to stick by these people of ours until we reach the clear, sure footing ahead."

The "storm" that Roosevelt referred to was the warfare that was dividing the nations of Europe and causing chaos in Asia. During his second term, Roosevelt had succeeded in keeping America out of the affairs of warring countries abroad. However, by 1940, it was becoming increasingly clear to the President that the

United States was destined to participate in the effort to combat the aggressive expansion of Germany and Japan. Though he hoped the United States would be able to remain neutral until the countries of the world reached that "clear, sure footing," Roosevelt doubted that peace could be secured while the United States stood aloof. He felt confident that he was the person best qualified to lead the nation and the world on the road to peace — and through a period of war, if necessary. Roosevelt asked the American people to give him their "vote of confidence" and reelect him to a third term. They did.

Relations between the United States and Japan had been difficult since July of that year, when the U.S. Congress passed the Export Control Act. That piece of legislation enabled the President of the United States to prohibit the sale and export of war equipment to foreign powers. The United States was determined to stay out of other nations' wars and claimed to be a neutral country. But the United States was in fact selling or leasing weapons and other tools of destruction to the participants in various armed conflicts around the globe, including Japan and Great Britain. When several governments questioned the supposed neutrality of a country so involved in the economics of war, Roosevelt and the legislators in the U.S. Congress saw the need to make U.S. trade policy consistent with U.S. foreign policy. First came the Export Control Act. Three months later, Roosevelt stopped the shipment of scrap metal to Japan, a move that country considered an extremely unfriendly act.

While the Germans strove to dominate Europe, Japan was aggressively pursuing its own policy of conquest and expansion in Asia and the South Pacific. It had already moved into China and northern Indochina, and was looking toward the Philippines. To emphasize its disapproval of such aggression, the United States put a further ban on all shipments of arms, petroleum products, machine tools, and raw materials to Japan. Great Britain and the Netherlands followed the United States by renouncing their own trade policies with Japan. Then, on September 27, 1940, Japan, Germany, and Italy signed the Tripartite Pact, which committed Germany and Italy to join Japan in any war against the United States.

Because Japan had relied on a steady stream of American weapons and raw materials to sustain its war machine, the U.S. government's refusal to supply these materials left Japan in an uncertain situation. Consequently, in March 1941 serious negotiations began between Japan and the United States. Though the object of the negotiations was to avoid war between the two countries, Japan continued to pursue its expansionist policies in Southeast Asia. In July, Japanese troops moved into southern Indochina, thus moving closer to the Philippines and trade routes important to the United States. The United States considered Japan's aggression against other countries and its threatening moves toward territory vital to U.S. interests inconsistent with any effort to negotiate terms of peace. In response, Roosevelt froze all Japanese assets in the

United States, effectively stopping all U.S. trade with Japan. The President also warned Japan that the United States would defend countries whose interests coincided with those of the United States.

In November, Japan seemed intent on reaching an agreement with the United States when it sent a special Japanese envoy to Washington to participate in negotiations. Japan's Prime Minister Fumimaro Konoye informally proposed concessions to U.S. diplomats that Japan would be willing to make in exchange for restored trade with the United States and U.S. economic aid. Konoye seemed willing to ignore some of the provisions of the Tripartite Pact in exchange for an end to the U.S. trade embargo. Some U.S. officials were slightly encouraged. However, Japan continued its aggression in Asia. In China, it supported a puppet regime, or one that was merely a front for Japanese control. At the same time, Japanese troop movement indicated a possible invasion of Singapore.

Roosevelt and his advisers did not trust Japan. They were also skeptical as a result of their dealings with Japan's Foreign Minister Yosuke Matsuoka. Matsuoka had a great deal of influence in the development of his country's foreign policy and had been very outspoken in his belief that it was in Japan's best interest to adhere to the Tripartite Pact. Through Japan's Ambassador Kichisaburo Nomura, Japan offered to withdraw its troops from China and to return nearly all the Chinese territory it had conquered back to the Chinese. In exchange, Japan wanted the United States to end its economic aid to

4

China, restore normal trade relations with Japan, and provide Japan with a loan, the amount of which was to be agreed on later. Though certainly not a leap toward peace, the Japanese proposal at least seemed to indicate a possible willingness to compromise for the sake of avoiding a war with the United States.

Months of talks ensued, but they were hampered by suspicions, language difficulties, and cultural differences, as well as by generally conflicting interests. Meanwhile, it became increasingly apparent that U.S. involvement in the war in Europe was inevitable. Germany, which had been steadily pursuing its own policy of expansion in Europe, had conquered several of its neighboring countries and was seeking to expand further. Outraged by Germany's brutal quest for world domination, the United States, on President Roosevelt's orders, began to strengthen its defenses and prepared for war. More proposals came from Japan, including a promise to end its expansionist policy and to withdraw its troops from Indochina. However, the Japanese demanded that in exchange the United States accept Japan's presence in China and other conditions the U.S. government considered unacceptable.

The talks stalled, and tensions between the two countries mounted. Nomura said to Roosevelt, "Your recent proposals will no doubt be the cause of painful disappointment to the Japanese government." Roosevelt replied, "To tell the truth, I too am very disappointed that the situation has developed in the manner that it has."

After what seemed like an endless series of offers and counteroffers, the United States offered Japan a policy declaration of its position on Asian affairs. The statement emphasized territorial integrity, equal commercial opportunities, and future security for all Asian nations. The Japanese were insulted and furious that the United States would dare to issue such a sermonlike declaration. Japan had already taken precautionary measures to prepare for war against the United States. Now, as relations between the two countries deteriorated beyond any possibility of reconciliation, Japan began to plan a first strike on the United States.

Roosevelt left Washington, D.C., the nation's capital, for Warm Springs, Georgia, where he often took vacations and spent time at a health spa. Only four days later he was called back as the Japanese threat to attack the United States became more imminent.

Roosevelt was kept abreast of developments virtually by the hour. Throughout its negotiations with Japan, the United States had listened to Japanese radio communications, deciphering complex codes so that Roosevelt, in his dealings with Japan, would know precisely what was behind that government's peace proposals. Now, potentially on the brink of war, the United States listened even more closely, hoping to intercept any information that might serve as a warning of an impending Japanese attack.

Roosevelt had been informed by his advisers that intelligence reports and intercepted Japanese radio messages seemed to indicate that Japan was planning to invade Thailand. Such an invasion would expand Japan's growing empire and would give Japan an additional strategic outpost. It would also damage the United States, which imported much of its tin and rubber from Thailand. Roosevelt and his advisers considered the question of whether, in the event of an attack on Thailand, the United States should intervene.

On December 3, 1941, Japanese officials in the United States, on the orders of their government, returned to Tokyo. On December 5, Roosevelt was told at a cabinet meeting that radio information regarding the movement of Japanese ships indicated that Japan was planning an attack on the United States or its territories and that any such attack would likely come from the south. (Additional messages were intercepted on December 6 — messages that would have revealed Japan's intention of bombing Hawaii — but these messages, because of their low priority classification, were not deciphered and translated in time to serve as a warning to the United States.)

President Roosevelt sent a personal letter to Emperor Hirohito of Japan requesting that he dispel the rumor that Japan was planning an attack on the United States. However, by the time Hirohito received the letter, it was too late to dispel any rumors.

Before dawn on the clear, calm Sunday morning of December 7, 1941, 189 Japanese fighter planes took off from aircraft carriers in the Pacific Ocean and made their way through the early morning darkness bound for Hawaii. U.S. military personnel stationed at Hawaii's Pearl Harbor naval base were either sleeping or performing their routine morning duties. Eight large American battleships were neatly moored in the harbor. Other vessels in the harbor or in dry dock included forty-one U.S. destroyers, eight cruiser ships, five submarines, and other smaller boats. One Navy officer later remembered looking up, before teeing off at a nearby golf course, and seeing the Japanese planes in the distance.

Just before eight o'clock that morning, the roar of sky bombers shattered the morning calm as every important military installation on the Hawaiian island of Oahu came under Japanese attack. Less than an hour later, another wave of Japanese fighter planes arrived to deal a second blow to the already devastated U.S. fleet. A third wave arrived, but the job was already complete.

In Washington, U.S. Secretary of War Henry Stimson, who was eating lunch at the time, received a telephone call from President Roosevelt. "They've attacked Hawaii! They're now bombing Hawaii!" the President shouted into the receiver. Stimson's reaction was one of both shock and relief: He never really believed that Japan would strike first, but now that it had, the United States no longer faced the decision of whether or not to enter the war.

The attack on Pearl Harbor took a tremendous toll in American lives and military equipment. Nineteen U.S. warships were destroyed, as were fifty-two U.S. fighter planes. More than 2,000 American sailors were killed, and 237 Army personnel lost their lives. Japan lost twenty-nine aircraft and six submarines, but, having caught America unprepared, it had, for the time being, wiped out the U.S. strategic presence in the Pacific in slightly less than two hours.

President Roosevelt was visibly shaken when he met with his cabinet at eight-thirty that night. Not only had the United States been attacked, but the U.S. Navy, a branch of the armed forces in which Roosevelt, a former assistant secretary of the Navy, had a great deal of pride, had been caught entirely unawares. The attack had resulted in the worst naval disaster in U.S. history. Roosevelt had a difficult time accepting the fact that the Navy had allowed itself to be so vulnerable to an air raid.

On Monday, December 8, President Roosevelt spoke to the American people from the rostrum of the House of Representatives. Looking out into the crowded chamber, he began, "Yesterday, December 7, 1941 — a date which will live in infamy — the United States of America was suddenly and deliberately attacked by naval and air forces of the Empire of Japan." He asked Congress to declare "that since the unprovoked and dastardly attack by Japan . . . a state of war has existed between the United States and the Japanese Empire."

The request made Roosevelt the second U.S. President in the twentieth century to ask Congress for a declaration of war. Thirty minutes later, Congress declared war on Japan. Within a week, Japan's European allies, Germany and Italy, declared war on the United States. The U.S. entrance into World War II was complete. The "storm" that Roosevelt had spoken of in 1940 was raging more furiously than ever, and the "clear, sure footing" that the President so wanted for his country was going to be a long time in coming.

2

Not a Care in the World

Hyde Park, New York, is a sleepy little village nestled in New York State's beautiful Hudson River Valley, about eighty miles north of New York City. The Roosevelts were one of many wealthy families that made their home in the valley. The first Roosevelt came to America from Holland in the 1640s, when New York was still a Dutch colony. Generations of Roosevelts subsequently settled and prospered among the gentle hills along the Hudson. Franklin's father, James Roosevelt, a New York City lawyer and businessman, and his wife, Rebecca, moved into their seventeen-room, Hyde Park manor house on a rainy day in April 1867.

James was of medium height, but his slender physique and proud bearing made him seem taller. His hazel eyes exuded a special confidence, and his brown but graying muttonchop whiskers gave him a distinguished air. Rebecca was slightly plump and

11

could have been described as jolly, in contrast to her slim and rather stern husband. The couple had been married fourteen years when they and their young son, James Roosevelt Roosevelt, or "Rosy," as he was called, arrived in Hyde Park.

Springwood, as the house and its surrounding land came to be known, was in ill repair, so James and Rebecca immediately set about putting it right. They renovated the house, planted a vegetable garden, and even raised a few farm animals. Though they took frequent business trips, sometimes even to Europe, James and Rebecca were always glad to return to the comforts of their home in Hyde Park.

Over the years, by purchasing adjacent parcels of land, James increased the Springwood acreage from the original 110 to more than 1,000. Despite his often pressing business interests, he managed to find the time to spend many an afternoon surveying his lovely estate. He hunted, fished, and explored the banks of the Hudson in his small boat. He also enjoyed riding horses, and his skills as a horse breeder were known throughout the valley. One morning, James looked up from his writing table and noticed some birds nesting outside his window. He wrote in his diary, "I often wonder why men are satisfied to live all their lives between brick walls and thinking of nothing but money and the so-called recreations of so-called society when there is so much enjoyment in the country."

Paradise was soon lost as Rebecca's health began to fail around 1870. She had gained an excessive amount of weight, suffered from chest pains, had trouble breathing, and was generally weak and unmotivated. Seeing his wife in such a state, James suggested that the family take a trip to Europe. They visited England, France, and Italy. Rebecca spent some days at a French health spa, where she took mineral baths and received various medicinal treatments, but nothing helped. The family returned to Hyde Park, and Rebecca's condition worsened. Years went by, and Rebecca's symptoms became more and more serious. In August 1876, James, troubled by his wife's grave condition, took Rebecca for a cruise aboard his yacht, hoping that the fresh salt air and warm sun would help revive her. However, Rebecca suffered a massive heart attack on the yacht. She was rushed back to New York City, where the Roosevelts had a home in Greenwich Village. Doctors were unable to help her, and she died there on August 21, 1876.

After his wife's death, James Roosevelt decided to spend some time traveling rather than return immediately to his home, which he knew would seem so empty without Rebecca. He visited friends in England and wandered about Spain and France for nearly a year. Rosy, now at Columbia College in New York City, continued his education during this time. James was now in his fifties and no doubt expected to live the rest of his life as a widower. A return to Springwood, he thought, with all the memories it held, was out of the question for the time being. He intended to return there eventually, to enjoy his retirement in naturally beautiful and familiar surroundings, but for now travel suited him best. He returned briefly to the United States in 1877, but was soon off again, to the Pyrenees mountains in the south of France. He spent nearly three years there among the majestic, snow-covered peaks. When he returned, in 1880, he attended a dinner party in New York City. It was there that he met Sara Delano.

Sara Delano came from a well-to-do merchant family much like the Roosevelts. She and her sisters were well known in New York social circles. The Delanos lived in Algonac, just outside of Newburgh, New York, across the river and about twenty miles south of Hyde Park. Because Warren Delano, Sara's father, had been a merchant who moved about the globe constantly, the Delanos had lived and traveled in many exotic places, including China and Egypt. Sara had studied in France and Germany and had known only the finest of life's offerings. She studied with excellent tutors, played piano, and was fluent in French and German. She was exceedingly cultured and well-mannered. Also, she was beautiful and graceful. James seemed to fall in love with her the moment he met her.

Sara Delano's first visit to Springwood, in April 1880, was a delight for both her and her host. James courted her in the traditional style of the landed gentry. They took carriage rides and leisurely strolls along pretty country roads. He showed her the valley from his small river boat, and they sat and enjoyed afternoon tea on the porch. It was that April at Springwood that the two agreed to be married. At twenty-six, she was little more than half James's age, but neither doubted they were suited to each other.

Franklin Delano Roosevelt and his father posed for this formal portrait in 1887. The Roosevelts were one of New York State's wealthiest and most prominent families. The young Franklin grew up with private tutors, frequent travel, and many other privileges not known to others.

Once Warren Delano's blessing was secured — not the easiest of tasks because of his generally stubborn nature — the wedding date was set for October 7.

The wedding at Algonac was a grand affair, with ferns, palms, and wildflowers throughout the house and on the grounds. Many guests came to the wedding from New York City by ferry. They arrived at Newburgh and were met by a fleet of Delano carriages ready to transport them to the family estate. A social event much written about in the New York papers, the wedding was not without its critics. Some expressed their dismay that such a lovely young woman had married a man twice her age. After the reception, the coachman snapped his whip, and the newlyweds were happily off to Springwood to begin their life together.

The couple spent a month in Hyde Park before leaving for an extended European honeymoon, during which they visited Italy, France, Spain, Holland, Switzerland, and England. By the time the Roosevelts returned from their travels, Sara was four months pregnant.

On January 30, 1882, after a long labor and a very difficult delivery, Sara gave birth to a ten-pound baby boy. The birth was so difficult, in fact, that the doctor had thought it unlikely that both baby and mother would survive. (It has been suggested that the painful and uncertain birth accounts for the unshakable bond that existed between Sara and her son throughout their lives.) After some debate, the baby was christened Franklin Delano Roosevelt.

From the front porch of his family's manor house

during the spring and fall, the young Franklin could behold the splendid rustic countryside that surrounded Springwood. Grazing sheep and cattle, orchards of fruit trees, flower gardens, and farm houses dotted the lush, colorful landscape. Occasionally, Franklin would spot a neighbor walking on a distant hill or catch a glimpse of a hawk as it swooped down on a field mouse. In winter, he would watch through a window as his neighbor's horse-drawn sleigh crossed a nearby snowy meadow, eventually disappearing around a bend.

As a child born to extremely wealthy parents, Franklin grew up enjoying every privilege and opportunity imaginable. By the time he was fifteen he had been to Europe eight times with his parents. The family also made frequent business trips to New York City and various other parts of the country. When Franklin accompanied his parents on such trips, as he usually did, they always traveled first class. This often meant private railroad cars and exclusive hotels in which their each and every need was tended to by servants. Sometimes they would be guests at the homes of James Roosevelt's wealthy business associates. Because his parents associated only with the world's social elite, Franklin very rarely had contact with working people, and even then only with servants, who were always especially well mannered when in the company of a Roosevelt.

Each summer the Roosevelts retreated to Campobello Island, a small Canadian island off the coast of Maine, where they kept a third residence. There Franklin learned to swim, fish, and hunt. He spent long hours exploring the island's wooded acres and boating off its rocky coast. His father often took him out on his yacht, and by the age of six Franklin had already learned the basics of yachtsmanship.

As his mind matured, Franklin began to spend his idle time indulging in hobbies. When he was nine years old his mother encouraged him to start a postage-stamp collection, believing that such a hobby would teach the boy to be neat and ordered and that these traits would carry over into manhood. Franklin enjoyed the hobby so much that he continued to collect stamps for the rest of his life, eventually filling 150 albums with more than one million stamps. Franklin also became interested in woodworking and was soon building toy ships and birdhouses, reflecting quite early the enthusiasm for boating and wildlife he would display throughout his life. He became an avid bird-watcher, making extensive notes on the behavior of local species from season to season. When Franklin was eleven, he wrote an essay, "Birds of the Hudson River Valley," in which he described many of the varieties of birds he had observed growing up in Hyde Park.

Franklin also developed a keen interest in photography, which during his youth was a relatively new invention. Photographic equipment was expensive and hard to find in those days, but these were no obstacles for a Roosevelt. Franklin purchased a Kodak camera and a tripod for an amount that many working people would have called several months' pay. He proceeded with wild enthusiasm to photograph virtually everything in sight, taking countless family portraits, still lifes, and nature photographs.

Horses interested Franklin perhaps more than any of his other pastimes. As a very young boy he was fascinated by his father's stables, and by the age of four Franklin was a skillful rider. Each morning, James Roosevelt would saddle up one of his horses and Franklin would mount "Debby," his Welsh pony. On a good day, they would ride as much as twenty miles together, often all the way to Algonac. Franklin and his father became very close. While Sara loved and doted over her "dear little man," as she called the boy, James became a role model as well as a respected authority figure for his son.

The Roosevelts continued to travel frequently, and in the winter of 1887 they spent eight weeks in Washington, D.C. During their stay in the nation's capital, the Roosevelts visited the White House and were received by President Grover Cleveland, whom James had helped get elected president three years before by making generous campaign contributions. They saw all the sights by day — the Capitol building, the recently finished Washington Monument — and socialized by night, dining with senators and congressmen and others who held important government posts. At the end of their stay the Roosevelts returned to the White House to say goodbye to the president. The chief executive, who during his term had begun to show signs of fatigue, said to Franklin, "I am making a strange wish for you. It is that you may never be president of the United States."

In 1890, James Roosevelt suffered a mild heart

attack, but he quickly regained his health. Only a year later he purchased a fifty-one-foot yacht, and, with the help of a small crew, was back to sailing. He called the ship *Half Moon,* after the vessel used by English navigator Henry Hudson, who explored the "New World" in the early seventeenth century.

Like the young aristocrats of Europe, Franklin received his early education from private tutors and governesses, of which he had at least eight during his boyhood. Of the many subjects Franklin studied, he especially liked history, geography, and foreign languages — French and German in particular. Franklin was a hardworking pupil and, to the delight of his parents, earned the praise and respect of his tutors.

Franklin was also a book lover. His mother often read to him, and *The Swiss Family Robinson* became one of their favorite books. He spent hours as a child reading adventure stories, especially tales set on the high seas. Later, he began to read many different kinds of books. Because the family library at Springwood was very large, Franklin could roam freely through centuries of history and great literature. His mother did not advise him on his reading. She knew that the Springwood library contained only the finest books, so that anything Franklin selected would do him good. One afternoon, Sara Roosevelt found her son sitting quietly, reading through Webster's Unabridged Dictionary page by page. When she asked him what he was doing, Franklin explained that he was reading the dictionary because "there are lots of words I don't understand." When Franklin added, "and I am nearly half way through," his mother knew she had a very special boy on her hands.

In the autumn of 1896, Franklin, now fourteen, enrolled at the Groton School, a boys' preparatory school in Massachusetts. Groton students were all from very wealthy families, and were expected to go on to study only at the nation's best colleges. James and Sara Roosevelt found it difficult to send Franklin away to school, but they were confident that Franklin would receive an excellent education at Groton and that Groton's headmaster, Reverend Endicott Peabody, would take care of their boy.

3

Learning for Greatness

Headmaster Peabody once said, "The best thing for a boy is to work hard . . . to play hard . . . and then, when the end of the day has come, to be so tired that he wants to go to bed and go to sleep. That is the healthy and good way for a boy to live."

Life at Groton was true to Peabody's philosophy. There was a bell for everything. The first one chimed at six-forty-five each morning. Leaping out of bed, Franklin and the other eighteen boys in his class ran naked, clinging to towels, into a tiled shower room. This lack of privacy was disquieting for Franklin, and no doubt for the others as well, but their uneasiness soon gave way to routine. What was harder to get used to were the cold showers, which the headmaster considered necessary for a quick start to the day. Franklin, accustomed to warm baths at Springwood, dreaded the shock of the icy water on his body each morning.

A second bell called the boys to breakfast, another signaled the beginning of morning services at the chapel, and still another started each day's classes. At noon a bell announced that lunch was served. Classes resumed at one o'clock sharp. After a long day of lessons, the boys rushed out onto the playing fields to take part in various sports, which were required. Once they worked up a sweat and an appetite, it was time for another cold shower and supper, to which the boys wore starched white collars and ties. Then they were expected to do their homework in a common study area before saying evening prayers and heading off to bed. There was certainly never any time for "loafing," which the headmaster considered "the curse of American school life."

Franklin's sparsely furnished six-by-nine-foot room at Hundred House, with its bare walls and floors, reflected the regimen at Groton. Groton students, who had all grown up in stately, well-furnished homes, were stunned by their stark living quarters. There were no closets; clothes were hung on pegs. Each room had only a bed, a bureau, and a chair. Wall hangings were not permitted. The headmaster recalled finding one boy weeping on his first day at school. When he asked him what the matter was, the boy, sobbing terribly, responded, "Sir, there are no carpets on the stairs."

Franklin soon distinguished himself academically at Groton. Only one month after his arrival, he was fourth in his class. During his first year, Franklin studied Latin, algebra, English literature and composition, ancient history, science, and the Bible. He also studied Greek, but did not take a liking to it. Franklin ranked in the top quarter of students throughout his four years at Groton, and Headmaster Peabody later said he displayed "more than ordinary intelligence."

Academic success was not the only mark of distinction one wanted to achieve at Groton. Sports were also very important, and here Franklin had his share of difficulties. He was too thin for football, Groton's principal sport, and he had never been on a team of any kind. He tried boxing and then baseball, but soon proved too delicate for these as well. Golf and tennis were Franklin's best sports, but these were not highly regarded by his schoolmates, so Franklin participated at a minimum. Finally, he became equipment manager of the school's baseball team. Though very little status came with this position, Franklin took his responsibility seriously and ultimately took pride in his team's victories. He enjoyed playing an important role in the team's success, and his need to be in with his mates was satisfied. Still, he was disappointed that he was not actually able to compete in athletics, which were so much a part of life at Groton.

Groton boys understood that in addition to academic and athletic achievement, religious character was an important mark of individual distinction. Franklin was not lacking in this virtue. He joined the Groton Missionary Society, a group of Groton boys who performed various good deeds for the poorer people in the local community. Franklin played organ in small churches in the surrounding villages and delivered coal to the elderly in winter.

The society also sponsored a summer recreation camp for poor boys from the slums of New York and Boston. At this camp, situated on Lake Asquam in New Hampshire, Franklin taught these less fortunate boys how to swim and paddle a canoe. His participation in the missionary society was Franklin's first direct contact with the poor, and it made a lasting impression on him.

The year 1898 was a difficult one for the Roosevelts. In January, Warren Delano died from pneumonia. Though Franklin had loved his grandfather, he was more concerned about his mother's suffering at the loss of her father. He wrote to her from Groton, "I know you are heartbroken, but we must remember that he has gone to a better place [heaven] than this earth, and will be far happier there." Franklin attended his grandfather's funeral, but Franklin's father was not able to be there. His health, too, had not been good in recent months, and Sara had become increasingly concerned about him. The couple left for Europe in the hope that the mineral baths at a spa in Germany would improve James's condition. Soon after they arrived, however, they received news that Franklin had contracted scarlet fever. They boarded the first ship home, making the eight-day journey back to New York. By the time they saw Franklin, he had been treated in the hospital and had nearly recovered from his illness. Still, Sara took her son back to Springwood so that he could recover entirely under the care of a private nurse, the same one who had cared for her father during his last days.

Back at Groton in September 1899, Franklin

began his senior year. What a year it was! For one thing, he made the football team. He was only second squad, and rarely left the bench, but he was on the team nonetheless. Franklin also continued to improve his golf game and won several tournaments in which he competed against older players. Franklin's intelligence had always distinguished him from the other boys, and this had earned him both the respect and the envy of his schoolmates. Now he was being noticed in other ways. Younger boys looked up to him, and older boys were charmed by him.

However, Franklin was not free of hostility or jealousy on the part of his classmates, for he had a tendency to be somewhat smug and self-satisfied. As Roosevelt biographer Geoffrey C. Ward wrote of Franklin, "He may have known more than most boys about the bigger world beyond Groton, but they knew far more than he about being boys." Still, Franklin wrote to his mother, "Football bruises, afternoon teas, lack of sleep, gossip, and engagements come thick and fast . . . a glorious time."

During his final year at Groton, Franklin landed the part of Uncle Boppady in the senior class production of a W. S. Gilbert musical called *The Wedding March — An Eccentricity in Three Acts*. He was ecstatic. When the day of the performance arrived, Franklin won the audience's approval. Sara and James, who made the trip to Groton to see the opening, enjoyed the performance so much that they stayed to see the second performance the following night.

Prize Day, the day on which individual seniors

27

were recognized for their various achievements as Groton students, was held on June 24, 1900, for Franklin's graduating class. Franklin won the award for the best essay in Latin — a forty-volume set of William Shakespeare's plays. Sara could not attend the ceremony because of James's ill health. Though concerned about his father and disappointed that his parents could not be there, Franklin was elated. He had been accepted to Harvard College, the country's most prestigious university, and the future looked bright indeed.

By the time Franklin Roosevelt entered Harvard at the turn of the century, America had become a highly industrialized modern nation. New industrial machinery had altered the very structure of American society. No longer was the farm the backbone of the nation's economy. Rather, manufacturing was the wave of the twentieth century. The factory, most believed, offered the individual greater opportunity. To pursue this opportunity, many Americans left their farms behind for the nation's cities, where it was thought a more prosperous, secure life could be found.

Americans were not the only ones who were eager to reap the harvest of industrialization in the United States. Vast numbers of immigrants came to America, mainly from Europe, at the turn of the century. Some of these immigrants came in search of greater religious freedom. Many fled oppressive governments in their home countries and were attracted to American democracy, which guaranteed individual rights. Others, having known famine and desperate poverty, came to America in search of jobs. All were seeking a better way of life. Mainly because of this wave of immigration, the population of the United States more than doubled between 1850 and 1900, bringing the estimated number of Americans to more than seventy-five million.

The benefits of the modern age were many, and drastically changed the way people lived. New inventions such as the automobile and the telephone made possible transportation and communication that had barely been dreamed of fifty years before. Also, a new medium, the motion picture, began to provide news and entertainment for the masses. Countless other modern conveniences became part of American life as the Industrial Revolution steamrolled America into the twentieth century.

One reason for the great growth of industry in America was the abundant supply of cheap labor. Because most of the new arrivals were ex-farmers unfamiliar with factory work, there were many more unskilled workers available than there were jobs. Consequently, the men who owned the factories were able to hire workers for extremely low wages and offer little if any chance for an increase over time. Factory workers, poor from the start, had no choice but to work long days, often for as little as $1.50 per day. Many of the workers had families to support, but at such a low wage only a meager subsistence was possible. Women worked in factories for wages as low as $6 a week. Even children, the cheapest labor of all, were sent to work by their poor desperate parents — and hired by greedy employers. It is estimated that at least 1.7 million children under sixteen years of age worked in American factories during the Industrial Revolution. Though poor children also served as cheap labor in other countries, in "the land of the free" this was considered a national embarrassment.

Factory owners, however, did not seem embarrassed as they raked in huge profits on the work of cheap labor. Factory laborers not only worked for very low wages, they were also forced to do so in workplaces that were filthy, noisy, poorly ventilated, dimly lit, and extremely hot in the summer and cold in the winter. Because factory owners refused to improve these degrading conditions, many laborers became ill or suffered injuries. According to a report published by the Commission on Industrial Relations, 35,000 workers were killed in industrial accidents and 700,000 were injured in 1914 alone. Since workers' insurance and benefits had not yet been dreamed of, the more fortunate of these laborers depended on their families to help them survive these illnesses or injuries. Others who were not so fortunate died.

In 1900, one percent of the families in America controlled about ninety percent of the nation's wealth, while two-thirds of all New York City residents, mostly factory workers, lived in unsanitary, crowded, and run-down tenements. To many it seemed that free enterprise had run wild at the expense of common human decency and that "the land of opportunity" was just another land of exploitation.

The literature of the period depicted the squalid

conditions in which the American worker labored. In 1906, writer Upton Sinclair published *The Jungle,* a novel that laid bare the horrible working conditions in the meat-packing plants of Chicago. The book outraged the country and helped bring about stricter regulation of the meat industry. One of Sinclair's mentors was writer Jack London. In London's 1907 novel *The Iron Heel,* one of his characters strongly criticizes the free-enterprise system: "In the face of the facts that modern man lives more wretchedly than the cave-man, and that his producing power is a thousand times greater than that of the cave-man, no other conclusion is possible than that the capitalist class has mismanaged . . . criminally and selfishly mismanaged."

As Franklin Roosevelt, now eighteen years old, walked through Harvard Yard in his freshman year, his mind could not have been farther from the problems facing America's cities and the hardships of the working class. Harvard was, as it had been for more than two centuries, a college for boys from America's wealthiest families. When a boy graduated from Harvard he would most likely succeed in his profession or perhaps devote his time and energies to public life in order to shape a better world. The university was a place where boys' young minds were cultivated with the classics and where they were sheltered from the harsh affairs of the outside world.

Franklin quickly set about making his mark on Harvard College. Curiously, despite his many disastrous attempts to participate in contact sports at Groton, Franklin first tried to enter Harvard's athletic program, a very competitive one nationally. Exhibiting a wealth of determination, if not recklessness, he tried out for every athletic team at the school. Though Franklin was now six-foot one and a half inches tall, he weighed only 145 pounds, which was much too light for the varsity football team. He was not a fast enough runner for the track team, and he did not have sufficient upper-body strength to join the rowing crew. After what seemed like an endless series of rejections it appeared that Franklin had finally accepted the fact he was not cut out for varsity team sports.

Franklin majored in history and government, with minors in English and public speaking. The excellent preparation he had received at Groton enabled him to take advanced-placement tests. In fact, he was able to graduate from Harvard in three years instead of the usual four. He joined the staff of Harvard's undergraduate daily newspaper, *The Crimson,* and by his junior year was elected editor-in-chief. Though he was not as good a student as he had been at Groton, most often earning what was called the "gentleman's C," Franklin distinguished himself instead with his charm and gracious manner. He was handsome, cheerful, worldly, and extremely wealthy. He was also a distant cousin of Theodore Roosevelt, who, during Franklin's freshman year, had become president of the United States. Not surprisingly, others took notice of him and wanted to enter his world. He got involved in social clubs and had many friends. In a letter to his mother, Franklin wrote, "I am doing a little studying, a little riding, and a few party calls."

Then Franklin's father's health took a drastic turn for the worse. In late November 1900, Sara summoned Franklin and his older half-brother Rosy, who lived with his wife, Helen Astor Roosevelt, in Hyde Park, to the Roosevelts' New York City residence at 10 West 43rd Street. For several days, Sara and Franklin comforted James, who was now seventy-two, in a very weak state, and clearly living out his last hours. Rosy arrived on December 7, and this seemed to brighten the old man's spirits. The following day, James Roosevelt died. His body was returned to Springwood three days later for a simple burial.

Franklin stayed on at Springwood for several days to console his mother and to indulge in thoughts of his father. During those few mornings he and Sara went to James's grave at the churchyard and laid flowers around it. Several Delanos spent time with Sara during her period of mourning. She also received scores of condolence letters from friends in many parts of the world.

At his father's death, Franklin inherited an annual allowance of about $6,000. This was a truly remarkable sum considering that the average school teacher in 1900 earned only about $500 a year. Sara, now forty-six, received the Springwood estate. She had already inherited more than $1 million when her father, Warren Delano, died in 1898, so she was more than adequately supported financially for widowhood. To be closer to her son, Sara took an apartment near Harvard.

Despite his mother's new perch from which she could monitor his activities, Franklin continued to immerse himself in Harvard's social scene. Dinner parties and formal dances were commonplace for Harvard students, and Franklin, always invited, almost never failed to attend. He developed interests in various young debutantes, but none of the girls he met kept him occupied for very long.

Then one day Franklin met Alice Sohier. The Sohiers were respected members of Boston's high society. One of Franklin's friends had known the Sohiers for years and introduced him to Alice at her family's home in Boston. Franklin was struck by her beauty, though she was not yet sixteen, and began to visit the Sohier house regularly. He also visited the family's vacation home in Beverly, a quaint coastal town about fifteen miles north of Boston. Mr. and Mrs. Sohier liked Franklin very much, and so did Alice. Why wouldn't she?! Franklin was a Harvard boy, three years her senior, full of enthusiasm and ambition, and, of course, very rich. They saw each other steadily through Franklin's sophomore year, going to dances and dinner parties together.

In July 1902, Franklin took Alice for a cruise on his yacht. They discussed marriage, and Franklin told her that he wanted many children, perhaps as many as six. This may have spoiled the relationship, for Alice had been told by doctors that she would have trouble bearing children, even to the extent that it could be risky for her. They continued to see each other until October of that year, when Alice left for a tour of Europe. By the time she returned, both she and Franklin had developed other personal interests. Still, they remained friends.

On November 17, 1902, five weeks after Alice left for Europe, Franklin attended the New York Horse Show at Madison Square Garden. There he was saw his fifth cousin, Anna Eleanor Roosevelt, and after the show he took her and her companions out for dinner. He was intrigued by her, and that night he wrote about her in his diary.

Franklin saw Eleanor for lunch two weeks later and again for tea two weeks after that. At a New Year's celebration at the White House, Franklin and Eleanor dined with his cousin, and her uncle, the President of the United States, in the state dining room. Then, in January 1903, at a party celebrating Franklin's twenty-first birthday, Eleanor raised her glass to the guest of honor. Theirs was a budding romance, and they corresponded while Franklin was back at Harvard.

Franklin's diary reflects his feelings for Eleanor at the time, but Eleanor's is very discreet. In those days, it was considered in very bad taste for a woman to express her feelings openly about a man, even in a way so private as one's diary. It is known that she had always liked Franklin very much, and she later recalled one incident that endeared him to her.

Eleanor had had a difficult childhood. Her mother, an ill-tempered and frustrated woman who often beat her daughter, died when Eleanor was eight years old. Her father, an alcoholic, died two years later. Her grandmother and legal guardian, who like her mother was very strict and often severe with Eleanor, imposed very old-fashioned rules on her granddaughter's behavior. When Eleanor was fifteen, she went to a party at a relative's house. Eleanor's grandmother had made her wear a dress that was entirely inappropriate for a young woman of her age, particularly one of her maturity and intelligence. Terribly ashamed of her appearance — the dress would have been more suited to someone half Eleanor's age — Eleanor stood off in a corner at the party. She was having a miserable time and hoped not to be noticed. Suddenly a tall, handsome boy, Franklin Roosevelt, stood before her and asked her to dance. She took his hand, and from that moment on, Franklin was someone very special to her.

Their romance blossomed during the summer of 1903. In those days a young lady of society never traveled alone, particularly when visiting a young gentleman. Eleanor, with five escorts and her maid, left for Springwood in June for a three-day visit. The weather was rainy, and so they stayed indoors for nearly the entire time. Then, three weeks later, when the weather was better, she returned with five other cousins. They went for a hayride and took walks along the Hudson. For hours they lay in the shade of a large tree, escaping the hot July sun and talking quietly. One evening, Franklin took his guests on a dinner cruise on his yacht. He was at his very best, making the perfect impression, as he guided the vessel along the dark river. Lights from the mansions up beyond the cliffs mingled with the stars, adding to the already magical quality of the night. When it came time for Eleanor to leave, Franklin invited her to visit Campobello, and she said she would.

Eleanor arrived at Campobello, this time escorted

only by her maid, on September 28, 1903. It was a lovely stay, filled with walks through the countryside, picnics, and yacht cruises on the river. Eleanor and Franklin agreed to write to each other regularly during the coming months. In one such letter, Eleanor wrote, "I do so want you to learn to love me a little . . . for I have grown to love you very dearly during the past summer."

At a Roosevelt family gathering at Thanksgiving in 1903, Franklin told his mother that he was in love with Eleanor. It was "quite a startling announcement" for Sara. She considered her son and cousin Eleanor too young to marry — he was twenty-one and she nineteen — and asked Franklin to put off any official announcement for at least a year. She believed that this would be more than enough time for the young man's feelings to wear off. She also wanted Franklin to focus on his last term at Harvard and to begin preparing for his first year at law school. Franklin agreed to his mother's request, and they returned to the supper table.

Franklin and Eleanor corresponded by letter through the fall, and on December 1 he brought her to New York City to visit his mother. They both were aware that Sara was inclined to discourage the marriage, but they believed it was because she feared she might be losing her son and not because she thought they were too young, as she had said. They tried to reassure her that her role in Franklin's life would not be diminished but would be enhanced. She would be consulted often about married life, they said, since Franklin had no experience with marriage! Then, of course, there would be grandchildren for Sara to help with. These arguments did not persuade her, however, and she made some effort to prevent the couple from carrying out their plans. Despite Sara's protestations, however, Franklin and Eleanor Roosevelt officially announced their engagement in November 1904, soon after Franklin began his first year at Columbia University Law School in New York City.

The marriage took place at the home of a family friend on East 76th Street in New York City on March 17, 1905, St. Patrick's Day and Eleanor's mother's birthday. Endicott Peabody performed the ceremony. The bride wore a white satin gown that had been worn both by her grandmother and her own mother on their wedding days. The couple received nearly 400 wedding gifts, and some 200 guests were in attendance. Flowers were everywhere. President Theodore Roosevelt gave the bride away, and as he did he said to Franklin, "Well Franklin, there's nothing like keeping the name in the family."

As the rice flew from all directions, Franklin and Eleanor were taken by carriage to Springwood, where they would spend their first week alone together. They delayed the start of their honeymoon until Franklin would be finished with his first year of legal study. Then, in June 1905, they set sail for Europe. As relatives of the president of the United States, Franklin and Eleanor received lavish treatment wherever they went. When they finally returned to New York City some three months later, they moved into a relatively modest house at 125 East 36th Street, which Sara Roosevelt had prepared for them, and Franklin began his second year of law school.

Franklin passed the New York State Bar examination after completing only two of the usual three years of law school. He decided not to finish his degree at Columbia. He had, to some extent, lost interest in practicing law. Though they had already begun a family — Anna, their first child, was born in 1906 — he and Eleanor had no pressing need to earn money. Together they had an annual income from trust funds that totalled more than $12,000, in those days quite a lot of money. Franklin began to fancy the idea of living a country squire's life, as his father had. When offered a position at a well-respected Wall Street firm in June 1907, Franklin accepted, but with little excitement.

While Franklin developed a specialty in admiralty law during the next five years, Eleanor gave birth to two more children: James in 1907, and Elliott in 1910, the year Franklin decided to enter politics.

4

Throwing in the Hat

Franklin Roosevelt was a registered Democrat. In 1910 this was unusual for a member of the wealthy class. Much as today, Democratic party policies in Roosevelt's time were generally aimed at giving the people of average or below-average means the best opportunity to better their economic condition. Republican policies were mostly aimed at maintaining the status quo, or things as they are. In the early twentieth century, with one percent of the families in America controlling ninety percent of the nation's wealth, the wealthy class had a vested interest in the status quo. Franklin Roosevelt registered as a Democrat not because he had visions of social reform and the sharing of wealth. Rather, he registered as a Democrat because his father had been one. Eventually, though, he would have such visions.

Roosevelt entered the race for state senator, nominated by New York Democrats from the twenty-sixth district, which consisted of Columbia, Dutchess, and Putnam counties. In his acceptance speech he said, "I accept this nomination with absolute independence. I am pledged to no man; I am influenced by no special interests, and so I shall remain."

No Democrat had been elected from the twenty-sixth district since 1856, but Roosevelt was not discouraged. For a month, he campaigned very hard, visiting local communities in a bright red touring car and making as many as ten or twelve speeches each day. Roosevelt would begin each speech with "My friends," making himself one of the people, and this opening eventually became one of his trademarks. Despite Roosevelt's wealthy background, the many workers and farmers of the Hudson Valley liked the would-be state senator and what he had to say. Still, because of the district's voting history, most experts felt Roosevelt could not win. He proved them wrong. Roosevelt received 15,708 votes to his opponent John Schlosser's 14,568.

Franklin and Eleanor arrived in Albany, New York's state capital, on January 1, 1911. During his two years in the state senate, Roosevelt proved himself a reform-minded legislator and an important party leader. In those days, like today, corruption was present at every level of government. Roosevelt was outspoken about the public's right to honest government. Always the lover of nature, he fought for a land-conservation bill that included regulation of the timber industry. The questions surrounding the passage of this piece of legislation brought to Roosevelt's attention a problem he would face the rest of his political career — the extent to which government could fairly regulate private industry. In March of that year, a tragic incident brought that issue into focus.

A shirt manufacturer called the Triangle Shirt-waist Company occupied the top three floors of a ten-story building in downtown New York City. Its employees were primarily girls and young black women. On March 25, a cigarette ignited some paper patterns that the company used in the manufacture of shirts. The fire spread and was quickly out of control. Most of the other businesses in the building were closed that day, it being a Saturday, and most doors leading to staircases were locked. By the time the Triangle workers became aware of the fire, they were in great danger. When they realized that they were locked in, they panicked. Rather than be burned alive, people began to gather on window ledges, but the ledges were too narrow. Forty-seven employees fell from the windows to their death, and another hundred died inside.

It was the worst industrial tragedy in the city's history, but the building's owner was not held legally responsible. There were no laws requiring building owners to take any fire-safety precautions. In addition, the Triangle Shirtwaist Company had not supplied safety insurance for their workers, so the families of the fire victims received nothing.

The Triangle fire made it clear that the safety of workers in America's factories depended on government regulation of industry. Employers could not go on making huge profits while putting workers at risk.

43

The public, outraged that the country's system of free enterprise could claim the lives of 147 workers, demanded legislation.

On June 30, 1911, a New York State Factory Commission was formed to investigate factory conditions around the state. They found unsafe machinery, records that had been altered to hide workplace hazards from Labor Department inspectors, and children working along with their parents, often for as many as nineteen hours a day. Fire escapes were usually missing or inadequate. The legislature quickly set about creating laws that would improve safety in the state's factories, end the use of women and children as cheap labor, and make employers supply accident insurance for workers.

Roosevelt played no role in the commission's investigation or its recommendation of new legislation. He had never understood the complexities of labor issues or the concerns of working people. When a bill that would limit the workweek for boys under twenty-one to fifty-four hours and for women to fifty hours came before the legislature, Roosevelt failed to push for it. It was not that he was entirely unsympathetic. He wanted to do things for workers. But he looked on organized labor, the workers' effort to change their own lot, as unpleasant and even somewhat nasty. When he witnessed workers joining in boycotts to force concessions from their employers, Roosevelt naturally sided with the factory owners. As a child he had been taught absolute obedience to authority and that rebellious behavior was inconsiderate.

But by 1912, perhaps as a result of the Triangle

Shirt tragedy, Roosevelt had become more sensitive to the urgency of the labor movement. When the fifty-four-hour bill finally came up for a vote, Roosevelt supported it. He also supported a workmen's-compensation bill and led an investigation of the Adirondack iron mines, where it had been reported that workers labored in extremely hazardous mine shafts. That year, as a result of his newfound sympathies toward labor, Roosevelt won reelection with the support of the New York State Labor Federation.

Also that year, Woodrow Wilson was elected president of the United States. Roosevelt had first met Wilson a year before. The state senator had supported the New Jersey Democrat in his bid for the Presidency, and had even tried, though unsuccessfully, to rally support for Wilson among New York State legislators. On March 4, 1913, Franklin and Eleanor attended Wilson's inauguration in Washington, D.C. That day, Roosevelt met Josephus Daniels, whom Wilson had appointed secretary of the Navy. When Daniels invited Roosevelt to become assistant secretary of the Navy, Roosevelt proudly accepted. "All my life I have loved ships and been a student of the Navy . . . and the assistant secretaryship is the one place, above all others, I would love to hold." On March 21, 1913, Franklin Roosevelt, now thirty-one, was sworn in as assistant secretary of the Navy, the youngest in U.S. history.

It is interesting to note that Franklin Roosevelt's political career unfolded in much the same way his cousin Theodore's had. Theodore Roosevelt also began his political life by serving two years in the

45

New York State legislature. He, too, left his seat at the state house to become assistant secretary of the Navy, in 1897. Now, Franklin Roosevelt not only placed his foot on the step previously occupied by his cousin, but he began to confide in friends that he might someday be interested in following his cousin's footsteps to the White House.

As assistant secretary of the Navy, Franklin Roosevelt inspected ships and naval stations and held them to exacting standards. He was filled with pride as he was welcomed aboard each ship. It was not uncommon for him to receive a seventeen-gun salute on such occasions. The sailors stood at attention and the officers were in full dress whites as Roosevelt walked among their ranks. He loved to sail on the fighting ships, especially the destroyers because of their speed and the ease with which they could be handled. He impressed officers and sailors alike with his thorough knowledge of ships and sailing. "I get my fingers into everything," he said, "and there is no law against it."

The new assistant secretary of the Navy instituted a number of important changes. Shocked to discover that many sailors were nonswimmers and that in the past several had drowned at sea, Roosevelt ordered that all sailors pass a swimming test before boarding ship. He reorganized the Navy bureaucracy, efficiently managing each department's time and money. He negotiated many Navy contracts with private firms, particularly for necessities such as coal, steel, and oil. In doing so, Roosevelt always kept minimizing waste foremost in his mind, thus making many sound deals within the Navy's budget. In general, Roosevelt was bent on making the Navy better than it had ever been, and to a large extent he succeeded.

Meanwhile, Washington society loved the Roosevelts. Franklin had uncanny social poise. His good looks and robust personality drew people to him. He was articulate and knowledgeable on many subjects. He was spontaneous, had a keen wit, and exuded an air of great confidence. Never overbearing, he was courteous, attentive, and genuinely interested in what others had to say. Eleanor, too, was intelligent and gracious, and was warmly accepted into Washington society. They seemed the perfect couple and, many believed, quite suited to be president of the United States and First Lady.

Eleanor gave birth to a son, Franklin, Jr., in 1914, and, with the Roosevelt children now numbering four, the family was a real clan. How they loved their father! Despite his incredibly demanding schedule, Roosevelt was always there to take part in family outings, usually initiating a game or a hike in the woods. Like his father had with him, Franklin took his children, whom he lovingly referred to as "the chicks," swimming, sailing, and horseback riding.

In 1914 war broke out in Europe. On June 28, Archduke Franz Ferdinand, the heir to the throne of the Austro-Hungarian Empire, was assassinated by a Serbian nationalist. A month later Austria was at war with Serbia, and soon thereafter the rest of Europe joined in the fighting. Russia came to the aid of Serbia, and Germany moved its troops in to support Austria.

In August, Germany declared war on Russia and on France, which had sided with Russia. Germany invaded Belgium on August 3. Great Britain, which had a treaty obligation to defend Belgian neutrality, declared war on Germany. Before long, virtually all of Europe was entangled in conflict.

Through all of this the United States remained neutral. Noninterference in European military conflicts had been U.S. policy since 1823, when President James Monroe presented his Monroe Doctrine to Congress. In 1916, President Wilson, who had campaigned for reelection as the man who had kept the United States out of war, was reelected to a second term. By 1917 the United States was involved in World War I, drawn into the conflict by many things. Among these were the German sinking of the British ship *Lusitania* in 1915; propaganda portraying Germany as a ruthless, barbaric country bent on conquering the world; and the destruction German submarines had carried out on navy vessels belonging to France and Great Britain. In addition, it appeared likely that Russia would be forced to withdraw from the war because of great domestic turmoil. It seemed to Wilson that the United States was needed in order "to make the world safe for democracy."

The U.S. war effort was massive. President Wilson authorized government control of many private industries so that their resources could be used to support the military. Roosevelt's responsibilities as assistant secretary of the Navy increased as he became involved in making many high-level decisions.

There was a belief that the Navy had to be strengthened for battle — more ships had to be built and more men had to be recruited — and Roosevelt energetically took up the task. He instituted a broad Navy modernization program and became obsessive about efficiency. As assistant secretary of the Navy, Roosevelt received excellent training for the high-pressure demands of a national crisis. It was the kind of experience one needed for the Presidency, to which he now openly began to aspire.

During the war years, Franklin and Eleanor spent a great deal of time apart. She had given birth to another son, John, in 1916, and was extremely occupied with her children either in Washington or in Campobello. Franklin spent a great deal of time away, increasingly busy with the business of the Navy in wartime.

The war ended in November 1918, with America's relations with Europe changed forever. No longer was Europe "over there," as one popular song of the time termed it. Now there was an active link between the United States and the countries it had helped triumph over German aggression. Roosevelt visited France and Germany to survey the toll the war had taken on these countries. President Wilson traveled to Versailles, France, to attend the international peace conference there in 1919.

Wilson received a hero's welcome from the French people at Versailles. He met with the other members of the "Big Four" — Prime Minister David Lloyd George of Great Britain, French Premier Georges Clemenceau, and Premier Vittorio Orlando of Italy.

He also met with delegates from thirty-two other countries. The Treaty of Versailles, arrived at after months of negotiations, proposed (among other things) the formation of the League of Nations, an international community whose members would vow to defend each other in time of war. Having witnessed the devastation that had been the result of World War I, the leaders of these nations were determined to avoid any future war. They believed that the formation of the League would create an alliance of countries with similar interests that would be so powerful militarily that no adversary would consider waging war against it.

When Wilson returned from France, his task was to rally support for the treaty and for U.S. membership in the League of Nations. He traveled across the nation to appeal to the American people. He urged them to contact their congressmen, who would have to vote on the treaty's ratification. He told the people that if the treaty failed to be ratified he could "predict with absolute certainty that within another generation there will be another world war." While on this tour, Wilson suffered a stroke and had to abandon the effort. As he recovered, the debate as to whether the United States should join the League raged on.

Roosevelt returned from his trip to the battlefields and ruined cities of Europe strongly believing that another European war would be disastrous. He therefore supported U.S. membership in the League of Nations as an expression of America's willingness to play an active role in world affairs and particularly in working toward a lasting peace. He believed, with

Wilson, that the world was counting on the United States to lead the effort and that another world war had to be avoided.

In March 1920, because of fierce opposition in the Senate, general uneasiness among the American people, and Wilson's unwillingness to compromise on a number of its provisions, the Versailles treaty was rejected by the legislature. The United States did not join the League of Nations. It remained to be seen if Wilson's prediction of a second world war in the next generation would come true. Still, for his work on the treaty, Woodrow Wilson was awarded the 1919 Nobel Peace Prize in December of that year.

That summer, Roosevelt was a delegate to the Democratic National Convention. The Democratic party, as it met in San Francisco to nominate its candidates for president and vice-president, was worried about its prospects for the coming election. President Wilson's illness had drained the President of his energy. In addition, his failure to win the legislature's approval of U.S. membership in the League of Nations had caused his political influence to dwindle. Yet there was no clear choice for a new leader to lead the party out of its confusion. When the delegates were counted, the party had chosen Governor James M. Cox of Ohio to run for president.

Of all the possible candidates for vice-president, Cox had expressed a preference for Roosevelt. "He met a geographical requirement," Cox said. Roosevelt was also "recognized as an independent" and had "a well-known name." Roosevelt himself had not expected to be considered for the nomination, but leading Democrats perceived him as the obvious choice. A surprised Franklin Roosevelt, now thirty-eight years old, was selected as Cox's vice-presidential running mate.

Though Roosevelt had been ill during the previous months with pneumonia, tonsillitis, sinus trouble, and various colds, the nomination filled him with enthusiasm and energy. He resigned his post as assistant secretary of the Navy and began preparations for a difficult campaign.

As he had done in his effort to be elected to the state Senate, Roosevelt campaigned with unflagging energy. In his many campaign speeches across America, he stressed many of the themes he had put forth in his campaign for the House of Representatives. He impressed the voters as a man who was on their side. He voiced his concern for land conservation and the plight of poor Americans, many of whom were living in crowded tenements and working in unsafe conditions for meager wages. He spoke out against child labor, and he stood by his belief in the need for an international community such as the League of Nations to deter the countries of the world from going to war.

However, the League of Nations issue proved a ball and chain for the Democrats. The Republican nominee, Warren G. Harding, a former Ohio newspaper publisher and one-term senator, won the election with 404 electoral votes to Cox's 127. He and his running mate, Calvin Coolidge, won not only the lion's share of the electoral college, but also received sixty-one percent of the popular vote and carried thirty-seven states. It was the largest margin of victory in a presidential election in a hundred years. Roosevelt sent a message of congratulations to vice-president-elect Calvin Coolidge and issued a public statement urging all Americans to join together to support the newly elected administration.

Still, though the Democrats had lost the election, Roosevelt knew that he had gained a great deal. Not only had he become acquainted with the realities of national political life, but he had also met a good many people on the campaign trail. Many of these would prove extremely influential when Roosevelt made his bid for the Presidency.

5

Journey to "Hooverville"

The 1920s were years of great cultural change in the United States. The horror of World War I had caused some Americans to question the traditions previous generations had held dear, such as religion, family, and country. They were eager to discover or create new values on which to base their lives and journeyed, so to speak, through life in search of ground on which to build a new beginning.

The Roaring Twenties, as that decade came to be known, was also a time of great economic expansion in America. Businesses flourished. There was enormous growth in the stock market. The production of consumer goods reached an all-time high. Americans enjoyed the good times and believed the prosperity would never end.

The decade also saw many extreme social practices gain acceptance, as personal freedom was stretched to new limits. Women's fashion trends in particular reflected the liberal era. Skirts were shorter, necklines were lower, and stockings were rolled down, exposing skin that even on the beach had never seen the light of day. Women wore makeup outdoors, shocking those with more conservative tastes. Women also stopped wearing corsets, which for them had become a symbol of enslavement. There was a surge in nightlife, as people flocked to wild parties and dance halls. The high ideals of the Wilson era were quickly — and even bitterly — thrown out. A gay decadence took hold of the country.

The great thinkers and writers of the time characterized the decade as one in which traditions had less meaning. Ernest Hemingway, for example, wrote novels and short stories about young, disenchanted Americans. His characters drifted aimlessly through Europe after World War I, having lost all faith in society and the possibility of finding a place for themselves in it. Another writer of the period, F. Scott Fitzgerald, wrote about the era in novels such as *This Side of Paradise* and *The Beautiful and Damned*. His characters, mostly people of considerable wealth, found themselves unable to give meaning to their lives.

It seemed to many that the former heroes of the Wilson era had been rejected along with its ideals. The democratic party had lost the election of 1920. Former President Wilson, who had taken the defeat of the Cox–Roosevelt ticket as a rejection of him and what his administration had stood for, retired to a house in a quiet Washington suburb. Roosevelt, however, was not ready to end his political career just yet. He went up to Campobello in the summer of 1921 to plan his next move — and to do a little fishing.

In August, however, Roosevelt began to experience symptoms of an illness unlike anything he had ever known. At first he thought he had only a bad cold — chills, fever, and a touch of rheumatism. The family doctor prescribed bed rest. Then, Roosevelt began to experience a loss of feeling in his legs, intense pain in his back, and dangerously high fevers. By August 12 he was unable to stand or even move his legs. Specialists were called, and each diagnosis was different. Then a doctor named Robert W. Lovett was summoned from his Boston office. After a thorough examination, Dr. Lovett diagnosed Roosevelt's illness as a form of infantile paralysis called poliomyelitis, or, simply, polio.

Polio is a viral infection that attacks the nervous system. In the early 1900s, doctors were barely familiar with the virus. There were polio epidemics on record, but even so the virus had proven only very mildly contagious. There had also been a noted recovery rate in a good many cases. Scientists, particularly one named Jonas Salk, would later develop a vaccine against polio in the 1950s. In the 1920s, however, Roosevelt could only hope for the best. Doctor Lovett prescribed hot baths and some medication to help the patient sleep, but there was nothing else he could do. Roosevelt was moved to a New York hospital and placed in the care of Dr. George Draper, a former schoolmate of Franklin's and a close colleague of Dr. Lovett's. There, Roosevelt was expected to recover in a few months.

On September 16, 1921, *The New York Times* carried a front-page story detailing Roosevelt's condition for the public. The report was overly optimistic, quoting Dr. Draper as saying Roosevelt "definitely would not be crippled." In truth, his pain became more intense each day. Even the slightest movement was extremely hurtful. In only two weeks, Roosevelt, a robust, thirty-nine-year-old husband and father of five young children, a public figure whom many considered a potentially great political leader, became a helpless prisoner in a body racked with pain. Still, Roosevelt believed his doctor's prediction and remained cheery, especially with Eleanor and the children when they visited. Before long, however, it became evident that there would be no recovery. On October 28, 1921, he was released from the hospital.

Though the pain subsided eventually, the disease had left Roosevelt's legs permanently paralyzed. He would never be able to walk again without the aid of leg braces and crutches. Even then he would only manage, with great effort, to take a few small steps at a time. As Roosevelt biographer James MacGregor Burns wrote in his book *The Lion and the Fox,* "The young man who had strode down convention aisles looking like a Greek god now had to be carried around like a baby, or pushed in a wheelchair. The man of only forty who had struck everyone with his animation and vitality spent hours crawling on the floor as he tried to learn to walk again."

Eleanor played a vitally important role at this point

Roosevelt reading about his re-election victory in the 1930 gubernatorial election in New York State. In 1921, Roosevelt had contracted polio, a viral infection that attacks the nervous system, which crippled him and forced him to wear leg braces known as callipers. Still, polio didn't stop him from taking powerful strides in his political career.

in her husband's life. She brought important political people to the house so that Franklin could maintain his contacts and made sure he received news of significant developments. She also tended to his more basic needs. Sara Roosevelt suggested that her son return to Hyde Park and live a retiring life in familiar, rural surroundings. Eleanor knew that her husband needed above all to go forward with his life. Through her support and good counsel she helped ease him back into the world of politics.

Still, it was Roosevelt's own courage that ultimately made his return to politics a reality. In fact, as he set about charting a rebound for the Democratic party from its 1920 defeat, Roosevelt exhibited an inner strength that impressed all who saw him during that difficult period and many historians since. His spirit seemed strengthened. His good nature had survived the physical agony, and his intellect was still keen.

Determined never to look as if he had been beaten by his condition, Roosevelt sustained a remarkable level of good cheer. He showed an uncanny ability for making the best of a horrible situation, certainly one that might have crushed a lesser person. Because he considered a standard wheelchair too imposing on others, Roosevelt designed a special wheelchair from a wooden kitchen chair, one that was better suited to the pleasant furnishings at Springwood. He had a pulley-operated elevator installed at the house so that he could transport himself to the second floor. He developed his upper-body strength and had long straps suspended from the ceiling so that he could move from his wheelchair onto other chairs or into bed without assistance. He had a car rebuilt so that it could be driven without using foot pedals. The vehicle was a prototype for those used by many handicapped people today. Though he had to wear heavy steel braces on both legs, Roosevelt learned to balance himself on his feet and eventually was able to walk very short distances on crutches. Thus, he was able to sit and chat with visitors, drive through town, or even stand at a podium or table without his appearance constantly reminding others that he was physically impaired.

Roosevelt found that the hot baths prescribed by Dr. Draper were an effective treatment for relieving pain and improving circulation in his legs. In 1924, Roosevelt visited Warm Springs, a health spa in Georgia, to bathe in the warm mineral waters there. He was immediately overwhelmed by the pleasant sensations he experienced simply by lowering himself into the swirling hot water. For hours each day he floated in the pool. Though certainly not a cure, the baths proved beneficial to both body and spirit.

Whether at Warm Springs or in Hyde Park, Roosevelt spent most days trying to regain some use of his legs. During the summer and autumn of 1922, for example, he struggled through a daily routine of strenuous exercise. This included "walking" with the aid of his crutches, building upper-body strength on the parallel bars, and swimming in a nearby heated swimming pool. At the end of each day he usually collapsed, exhausted, into his wheelchair. But he was making progress. As the weeks went by, he was able to cover greater distances. The distances in question were quite small, but even an additional step or two farther than he had gone on the previous day's outing was considered a triumph.

Many who knew Roosevelt, including Eleanor, have written that during this period he became a deeper, more philosophical person. The disease, they said, caused him to turn inward. It has been suggested that a new, more serious Roosevelt emerged as he faced the fact of his illness. Whether the effect of Roosevelt's illness on his inner life has been exaggerated or not, the effect it had on his political life was great. The courage Roosevelt displayed in the face of a horrible disease endeared him to the American people. Anyone who in the past might have considered Roosevelt merely a boy of privilege who had never known the sufferings of men did so no longer.

Roosevelt reentered national politics in June 1924 at the Democratic National Convention in New York City. He was scheduled to give a speech nominating New York Governor Alfred E. Smith for president. Woodrow Wilson had died in February that year, so the presence of Roosevelt, as the surviving bearer of the Wilson legacy, initially stirred mixed emotions among the convention's delegates.

When the time came for Roosevelt to address the audience, he very slowly made his way from the convention floor onto the speaker's platform. Despite his leg braces and crutches, it was still necessary for him to enlist the help of his son James, who was now a student at Groton. While his son walked closely by his side, Roosevelt clung to James's upper arm and dragged his useless legs inch by inch. The short walk was a great struggle for Roosevelt. The crowd, recognizing this, cheered wildly as he came into view. Roosevelt relaxed the tight grip he had on his son's arm, laid his crutches aside, and braced himself against the podium, perspiring and breathing heavily. As the delegates roared with approval and admiration, the well-known Roosevelt grin shone in the convention-hall spotlight.

When silence fell over the hall and every ear turned in his direction, Roosevelt nearly hypnotized the audience with his eloquent delivery. When he finished, the applause continued for what seemed like an hour. Never had a national convention witnessed such a display of courage and determination. Though the Democratic party ultimately nominated John W. Davis, a former ambassador to Great Britain, to run for president of the United States, in a very real sense Roosevelt emerged from the convention a winner.

Roosevelt continued to take regular trips to Warm Springs. As he struggled with his own ailment, he became increasingly interested in helping other polio victims. In 1926, Roosevelt bought the Warm Springs resort and began to renovate it for use by others in addition to himself. A year later he founded the Georgia Warm Springs Foundation, a nonprofit organization established to help victims of polio through treatment and counseling. He spent more than $200,000 on the renovation of Warm Springs, and eventually the spa became an international center for the study and treatment of polio.

Also during the 1920s, Roosevelt became involved

in various business ventures, worked for several foundations and charitable organizations, and did a great deal of writing, including book reviews and magazine articles. Though he resumed practicing law for a short time, he quickly gave it up. He considered himself more of a businessman and administrator than a lawyer.

At the 1928 Democratic National Convention, held on June 27 in Houston, Texas, Roosevelt once more endorsed and gave the speech nominating Alfred E. Smith for president. This time his son Elliott, now a student at Groton anticipating his freshman year at Harvard College, assisted Roosevelt, just as his son James had done four years before. It was another difficult trip to the podium, but Roosevelt was more at ease than he had been in 1924. Though not as inspiring as his 1924 speech, Roosevelt's endorsement of Smith, who was known as the "Happy Warrior," was well received. To enthusiastic cheers, he ended by lavishing praise on the governor of New York:

"America needs not only an administrator, but a leader — a pathfinder, a blazer of the trail to the high road that will avoid the bottomless morass of crass materialism that has engulfed so many of the great civilizations of the past. It is the privilege of democracy not only to offer such a man but to offer him as the surest leader to victory. To stand upon the ramparts and die for our principles is heroic. To sally forth to battle and win for our principles is something more than heroic. We offer one who has the will to win — who not only deserves success but commands it.

Victory is his habit — the happy warrior, Alfred E. Smith."

Smith won the nomination, but he immediately ran into trouble on the campaign trail. This came about, to a large degree, because of anti-Catholicism. There had never been a Catholic president, perhaps because many voters felt that Catholics in high office would have conflicting allegiances to the church and the country. When the polls showed that Smith was unlikely to carry his home state of New York, the Democrats began to doubt he had even the slightest chance of winning the election. Smith suggested that his longtime friend and supporter Franklin Roosevelt run for governor of New York to boost the Smith campaign in New York. It was thought that Roosevelt, popular in districts where Smith was weak, could help the Democratic line win votes there.

Roosevelt was eager once again to hold public office, especially another office once held by his cousin Theodore. But he hesitated to seek the governorship, mainly because of his health. He felt he had made progress by sticking to his daily exercise routine and his baths at Warm Springs. Hoping eventually to be able to walk with just a cane and braces, he wanted to keep up the regimen. Eleanor agreed that her husband should continue, for the time being, working to improve his health. In addition, most of Roosevelt's friends and political advisers suggested he wait. They wanted him to regain his health, of course, but they also wanted the Democrats to improve their standing with the voters, a reference to the weak Democratic presidential nominee, Smith.

Despite his hesitations, and against the advice of his family, close friends, and colleagues, Roosevelt agreed to accept the nomination of his party for governor of New York. He realized that without his candidacy the Democrats stood very little chance of winning the White House. Also, his sense of duty and dedication to public service drove him to accept.

Many political experts believed Roosevelt's illness would make it difficult for him to win the election. Voters, they felt, would look on Roosevelt as weak and crippled, unable to serve effectively as the state's chief administrator. Smith, however, put their doubts to rest. Speaking in 1928, he said, "Franklin Roosevelt is physically as good as he ever was in his life. His whole trouble is his lack of muscular control of his lower limbs. But a governor does not have to be an acrobat. We do not elect him for his ability to do a double back-flip or a handspring. The work of the governorship is brain work."

Roosevelt's campaign got off to an excellent start. He traveled by both car and train to every county in the state of New York, and spoke to large, receptive audiences. It was impossible to tell exactly how much Roosevelt's candidacy was helping the Smith presidential campaign. However, the overall prospects did not look very good. When the votes were counted, Herbert Hoover, not Smith, was elected President of the United States. Still, despite the Democratic party's failure to win the White House that year, at least one very important Democrat was victorious. Franklin Roosevelt, at age forty-six, was elected governor of New York.

On January 1, 1929, Roosevelt delivered his inaugural address, outlining some of his objectives as governor: "To guard the toilers in the factories and to insure them a fair wage and protection from the dangers of their trades; to open the doors of knowledge to their children more widely; to aid those who are crippled and ill . . . these great aims of life are more fully realized [in New York] than in any other state in the Union. We have but started on the road, and we have far to go."

Roosevelt had won by only a slim margin, but he gained instant national political recognition when he became governor. This is because many people considered the New York governorship to be a stepping stone to the White House. In fact, the office was considered a suitable training ground for the Presidency. New York was a large state with a diverse population, and so presented its governors with situations and problems similar to those a president would face. In addition, many former New York governors, particularly in the previous fifty years, had gone on to be nominated by their respective parties to run for president. Thus, when his name was mentioned as a possible future president, and when it was suggested that he might even run in 1932, Roosevelt did not discourage such talk.

Roosevelt proved to be a very able governor and one very interested in reform. During his first two-year term, he put the state finances in better order and made improvements in state health care. He also focused on two of New York's most urgent problems — the sorry condition of the state prison system and the lack of fairness in the state's worker's-compensation laws.

In July 1929, 1,300 inmates at Clinton State Prison rioted and set fires to protest prison conditions, particularly overcrowding. Three inmates were killed and many were injured in the clash with prison guards. Also that month, prisoners at the Auburn prison facility rioted and caused more than $200,000 worth of damage. In that incident, two inmates were killed. To relieve the overcrowding in New York State prisons, Roosevelt pushed for the building of another prison facility. The result was Attica, completed in 1930 at a cost of $12 million. He also oversaw the restructuring of the parole system, reinstated the policy of time off for good behavior that had been phased out by previous administrations, and developed programs whereby inmates could learn job skills they could use once they were released from prison. Moreover, Roosevelt saw that the criminal laws were made more lenient, and out of sheer compassion commuted to life imprisonment many death sentences that had been handed down.

The conditions of the state's workplaces were hardly better than the prisons when Roosevelt became governor. He quickly set about improving the lot of working people. More than half a million industrial accidents caused by unsafe working conditions were reported in New York each year during the early-to-mid 1920s. Injured parties were often unfairly denied compensation by corrupt employers. At the same time, greedy doctors who treated workers frequently pocketed compensation money beyond the cost of the actual treatment. Roosevelt pushed for the reform of workers'-compensation laws so that injured workers were less likely to be cheated.

As the 1920s came to an end, the American economy was at a peak. American industrial production was soaring. Americans were earning wages never dreamed possible a decade before. Businessmen, admired for making the United States the wealthiest, most powerful nation in the world, had become America's new elite. Employers urged their workers to invest their wages in stocks, and many people became rich seemingly overnight by doing so. An article entitled "Everybody Ought to Be Rich" was published in the *Ladies' Home Journal.*

But as the decade ended, so did the party. In October 1929, a sudden plunge in the stock market marked the beginning of the period in American history known as the Great Depression. Many experts expected the market to recover immediately. But as America moved into the 1930s, the Depression quickly worsened. Businesses went bankrupt. Factories across America closed and left workers without jobs. Farmers lost their farms. The nation's major industries, such as steel and automobile manufacturing, operated at a fraction of their capacity. Savings banks watched their deposits dwindle, and then closed. Families were forced to live off their hard-earned savings until the money was gone. A large class of hungry, homeless people emerged in America. Millions stood on line at soup kitchens or begged in the streets. Many men who could no longer support their families became hobos, riding from town to town on railroad freight cars, trying to find work, usually unsuccessfully.

Many blamed President Hoover for America's economic woes. Hoover was a staunch conservative and a *laissez-faire* capitalist, or one who believed that capitalism works best when it is unrestricted by any form of government regulation. Even in the face of a rapidly climbing unemployment rate — up to twenty-five percent by 1931 — the conservative Hoover refused to take executive action to put the nation back on its feet economically. His administration devised no plan and took no initiative to stimulate the economy. Rather, the President believed, capitalism would mend itself. In fact, Hoover seemed indifferent to the suffering of millions of Americans. While he stubbornly adhered to this point of view, America, hungry and out of work, begged for leadership.

Roosevelt, now serving in his second term as governor, characterized the problem in a 1932 speech: "We find two-thirds of American industry concentrated in a few hundred corporations, and actually managed by not more than five human individuals. We find more than half of the savings of the country invested in corporate stocks and bonds, and made the sport of the American stock market. . . . We find a great part of our working population with no chance of earning a living except by grace of this concentrated industrial machine."

Nearly thirteen million American men and women were unemployed. Soup lines seemed to be growing every day. Shantytowns known as "Hoovervilles" sprang up in American cities. In these small communities, people lived in shabby homes they built out of old cardboard boxes and other refuse. Many Americans picked through garbage heaps in search of food.

It was clear to the American people that the Great Depression would not go away by itself. They realized that the country would need real leadership in the White House to survive what was the worst economic depression in America's history. In 1932, an election year, most were ready to look to the Democratic party, and to one particular Democrat, for that leadership.

6

Birth of the New Deal

Franklin Roosevelt entered the 1932 presidential race on January 22 of that year. As governor of New York, he had shown himself to be a strong administrator who was willing to experiment with reforms aimed at breathing life back into the U.S. economy. He had become the first major political leader in the country to support unemployment insurance. He had openly criticized Hoover's conservative policies and lack of imagination. In a speech he gave at a governors' conference in June 1931, Roosevelt had pointed an accusing finger at the Republican administration:

"More and more, those who are the victims of dislocations and defects of our social and economic life are beginning to ask respectfully, but insistently, of us who are in positions of public responsibility, why government can not and should not act to protect its citizens from disaster. I believe the question demands an answer and that the ultimate answer is that government, both state and national, must accept the responsibility of doing what it can do — soundly with considered forethought, and along definitely constructive, not passive lines."

The Democratic National Convention that election year was to be held in Chicago in June. Roosevelt's aggressive campaign in the months leading up to the convention made him the leading candidate in a pool of many able contenders. He secured the delegates of the Southern and Border states. (Missouri, Kentucky, West Virginia, Maryland, and Delaware were known during the Civil War as "border" states because of their divided loyalties between the warring North and South.) However, Alfred E. Smith, once again in the race, managed to get a grip on a large portion of the New York delegates and all the delegates in Massachusetts, Rhode Island, and Connecticut. Meanwhile, Speaker of the House John Nance Garner of Texas claimed all of California's forty-four delegates, as well as forty-six from Texas. Still, after months of political maneuvering by all the candidates, Roosevelt emerged victorious.

In his acceptance speech, Roosevelt blamed the Republican administration for sitting by and doing nothing while the country's economy fell to ruin. He criticized Hoover for favoring the interests of big business over the welfare of the American people, and for adhering to an unproductive political philosophy when active, liberal thinking was called for. He also condemned the decadence of the wealthy and powerful, who Roosevelt believed had a moral obligation to act compassionately for the sake of the country.

"Today we shall have come through a period of loose thinking, descending morals, an era of selfishness among individual men and women and among nations," he said. "To return to higher standards we must abandon false prophets and seek new leaders of our own choosing." Roosevelt offered Americans a "New Deal" and promised "to restore America to its own people" if elected.

Roosevelt crisscrossed the nation campaigning. The main issue of the race was the state of the economy, so Roosevelt spoke to that issue at every campaign stop. He believed that capitalism had to be controlled in order to be effective. He pointed to the sad state of the U.S. economy to illustrate how capitalism, left unchecked, had led to the dominance of the greedy, aggressive few at the expense of millions of honest, hardworking Americans. Roosevelt said that it was inexcusable that the United States produced so much wheat and yet had so many hungry families. He expressed his anger at the fact that so many people were without jobs even when there was so much work to be done to build a better America. He promised to act deliberately with creative, liberal policies to bring prosperity back to America.

At their convention, the Republicans surprised most people by nominating Hoover for reelection. Hoover continued to oppose any policy that would further involve the Federal government in what he considered the affairs of private industry. He proposed a solution whereby the few individuals who continued to gather in the nation's wealth would, through voluntary cooperation, help the economy by creating jobs and training people for them. This led many people to believe that Hoover did not really understand how such things worked. Others considered him unfeeling. It seemed to most Americans that Hoover either had his head in the sand, unable to recognize the seriousness of the national economic crisis, or was determined to feather the nest of big business for as long as possible.

On Election Day, 1932, Roosevelt crushed Hoover, winning nearly 23 million votes to the Republican's 16 million. Democrats gained a significant majority in both the House and Senate as well. Hoover lost the electoral vote 472 to fifty-nine, carrying only six states. The people had spoken, and spoken loudly.

When Roosevelt took office on March 4, 1933, more than thirteen million Americans were unemployed, and the country looked to their new president for leadership during this difficult period. In his inaugural address, Roosevelt did all he could to rally the nation: "This great nation will endure as it has endured, will revive, and will prosper. So first of all let me assert my firm belief that the only thing we have to fear is fear itself — nameless, unreasoning, unjustified terror which paralyzes needed efforts to convert retreat into advance."

During his first hundred days in office, Roosevelt laid the foundation for his New Deal policies by forming numerous relief programs. All were aimed at reducing the number of people on unemployment.

He established the Federal Emergency Relief Administration (FERA), which provided direct financial assistance to unemployed individuals and families. Still an advocate of land conservation, he created the Civilian Conservation Corps (CCC). Between 1933 and 1941 the CCC employed 2.7 million men to work on environmental projects. Workers in the CCC received lodging and $30 per month.

Roosevelt reached out a hand to the nation's farmers, many of whom had lost their farms in the late 1920s, with the formation of the Agricultural Adjustment Administration (AAA). Also during his first hundred days, Roosevelt established the Tennessee Valley Authority (TVA). The TVA would oversee land and resource use in parts of Alabama, Georgia, Kentucky, North Carolina, South Carolina, Tennessee, and Virginia, where many farms had failed due to overproduction and dropping prices.

The nation's business leaders also received benefits from Roosevelt's New Deal. The President wanted to stabilize the economy and help restore confidence in the country's banking system. One way to do this, he felt, was to assure individuals that their bank accounts were protected from any wild changes in the stock market. Roosevelt set up the Federal Deposit Insurance Corporation (FDIC) to do just that. The Securities and Exchange Commission (SEC) was formed in order to provide prospective stock purchasers with accurate securities information on a given company. Roosevelt appointed his friend Joseph Kennedy, the father of future President John F. Kennedy, as the commission's first chairman.

77

Roosevelt won passage of the National Industrial Recovery Act, which was aimed at creating jobs and providing guidelines within which businesses could operate freely and profitably, yet fairly. The National Recovery Administration (NRA), created to administer the act, imposed various codes of fair competition on American business. The move had mixed results. The bill represented important steps toward abolishing child labor and establishing a national minimum wage. But the NRA bureaucracy proved unwieldy and its codes of fair competition were later ruled unconstitutional by the Supreme Court.

Concerned about the morale of the country as well as its industries and finances, Roosevelt carried on a regular dialogue with the American people throughout his Presidency. He gave a series of radio addresses in which he outlined his plans for the country. These became known as "fireside chats." Roosevelt firmly believed in government "for the people." This became evident as Americans across the country listened to his voice over the airwaves. Families and neighbors gathered around the radio when a chat was scheduled, eagerly anticipating Roosevelt's opening salutation, "My friends." They listened very closely as the President described his administration's policies. Roosevelt spoke in simple terms so that the average person could understand. This greatly endeared him to the American people, who came to feel almost as if they were getting to know their president personally. Roosevelt also held 337 press conferences in his first term — compared to Hoover's total of sixty-six during his entire term. This both put him in good favor with the media and gave the country a real sense of involvement with the workings of its government.

Still, at the core of Roosevelt's success with the people was his political philosophy, which was based on compassion and a sense of fairness. In a 1935 public address, he summarized this philosophy: "We have a clear mandate . . . that Americans must forswear that conception of the acquisition of wealth which, through excessive profits, creates undue private power over private affairs and, to our misfortune, over public affairs as well."

Pleased with the results he was seeing, Roosevelt continued to create relief programs in his first term. The Civil Works Administration (CWA) provided more than six million jobs in less than a year. Men and women across the country left the unemployment lines and went to work to repair roads and public utilities in the many communities that had badly deteriorated under the strain of the Depression. Delighted with the CWA's success, Roosevelt created the Public Works Administration (PWA) to help private industry help itself. The PWA awarded government contracts to private construction companies for the building of hospitals, libraries, and other public facilities. The Triborough Bridge in New York City, a new sewage system in Atlanta, Georgia, a ski lodge on Oregon's Mount Hood, and a library in rural Kentucky were just a few of the PWA's many successful projects.

In April 1935, Congress passed the Emergency Relief Appropriation Act, which allocated $4.8 billion for work programs. The Works Progress Administration (WPA), which replaced the Federal Emergency Relief Administration that year, put the money to good use, financing community improvement, restoration, and development, and training the people to do the work. The WPA provided the funding for more than 250,000 projects, including the building of hospitals and schools across the nation.

Many artists, musicians, actors, and writers also benefited from Roosevelt's New Deal policies. The Federal government funded concerts and commissioned murals for the walls of Federal buildings. Through the Federal Theater Project, a division of the WPA that ultimately employed more than three million people, the government also produced nearly 3,000 theatrical performances. Many Americans who had never before been to a theater performance saw WPA productions. During those years, folk singer Woody Guthrie popularized the agency in song, reflecting the good feeling that had begun to take hold of the country because of New Deal job programs.

Roosevelt's New Deal undoubtedly had many critics. But the majority of Americans admired and supported the President's bold efforts to reduce unemployment and stimulate the economy. He had exercised an enormous amount of power in his first hundred days, the likes of which had never been seen before. Indeed, many said he had, perhaps, changed the office of the Presidency forever through his actions. Many who cherished America's free-enterprise system felt Roosevelt had overstepped the bounds of the executive branch. Regardless, most Americans knew that without Roosevelt's initiatives, the nation's economy might have never recovered. The 1934 congressional elections indicated that the vast majority of Americans were happy with Roosevelt's New Deal. The Democrats dramatically increased their majority in the House and Senate by posting many key victories.

On July 5, 1935, another important piece of New Deal legislation was signed. The National Labor Relations Act, or the Wagner Act as it was commonly known, set guidelines by which workers could organize and bargain with their employers. It protected workers and their unions from unfair practices on the part of employers, and established the National Labor Relations Board to hear disputes under the act. The Supreme Court recognized the Wagner Act as constitutional in a 1937 decision.

As a result of the Wagner Act and the power it gave to labor unions, the number of workers belonging to unions increased significantly during the late 1930s. The labor movement in general moved ahead in leaps and bounds. America's largest industries, such as the auto and steel industries, quickly moved to unionize, and the Roosevelt administration continued to put forth legislation aimed at protecting the rights of workers.

Victories for the labor movement were hard won during the 1930s, as unions dealt with stubborn, often underhanded management and disagreements within their own ranks. Strikes were frequently met with union-busting tactics and even violence, as unsympathetic industrialists fought to deny workers the most basic rights. Despite this opposition, the labor movement, with the help of New Deal legislation, made great strides through the end of the decade. Perhaps more than anyone, Roosevelt was responsible for the workers' newfound dignity.

On August 14, 1935, Roosevelt gained congressional passage of the Social Security Act. The Social Security program taxed employers and employees to create a fund from which the unemployed and the elderly could draw a monthly allowance. It was an immediate and lasting success.

These policies and programs of Roosevelt's first term certainly did not bring an end to the Great Depression. But conditions had improved significantly during those years, and there was reason to look to the future with a degree of hope. The unemployment rate had dropped. Factory wages had increased. Workers were guaranteed their basic rights under the law. The unemployed and elderly were provided for. The economy was showing definite signs of life again, as farms and city businesses both began to prosper once more. Still, to many this renewal seemed slow in coming, while others felt what little improvement the country had seen had come at too great a cost. America would have its chance to voice its approval or disapproval of Roosevelt's first term when he made his bid for reelection. That race, in 1936, divided the nation like none before it.

7

The ABCs of Government

Roosevelt was confident he would be reelected in 1936. He had waged war on poverty, stimulated the American economy, joined hands with the American worker, and, perhaps most important, given the nation back its sense of pride. These were impressive achievements. Millions of Americans respected their president for his courage and decisiveness. He had stood nose to nose with the Great Depression, and the latter seemed to be backing down. His New Deal policies had exposed the darkness to the light of day, and America's future looked brighter because of his efforts.

Many were still critical of Roosevelt, however, and by now he had critics on both ends of the political spectrum. Conservatives believed government should stay out of the affairs of private industry. They criticized Roosevelt for interfering with America's free-enterprise system. Some even accused him of leading the country down the road to communism, a system based on property ownership by a community as a whole or by the state. Political radicals, on the other hand, considered capitalism to be the cause of the country's economic ills. They urged Roosevelt to move quickly to replace capitalism with another, more just system.

Roosevelt's position was in the middle ground. That is perhaps why he had so many critics among political pundits, while average Americans all across the country strongly believed in him.

At the 1936 Democratic National Convention, held in Philadelphia that June, Roosevelt was nominated to run again for president before a cheering audience. The reception was just as enthusiastic as he traveled along the campaign trail. In fact, it was clear to all who witnessed Roosevelt among the voters — giving speeches, listening, shaking hands — that he had become nothing less than a national hero. He visited small towns and cities, smiling and waving from his car. Onlookers cheered and held up signs proclaiming the success of the New Deal and thanking the president for all he had done to save America from the Great Depression.

As election day drew near, the Republicans, predictably, attacked Roosevelt and his New Deal policies. In their campaign speeches, they referred to the president as "Franklin Deficit Roosevelt," and accused him of trampling on the Constitution, overspending, and creating a welfare state. These charges were to some extent justified. Roosevelt had extended the constitutional powers of the Presidency to new limits. He had taxed America heavily to pay for his many costly social programs. He had created a large class of Americans who were dependent on handouts from the country's welfare system. Still, many people defended their president, pointing out that Roosevelt took office during a national economic emergency, a time when drastic measures were not only appropriate but necessary. All the polls predicted a very close race, and the Republicans knew they would need every vote to oust Roosevelt.

One measure of the feelings Republicans had for Roosevelt could be found in the party platform, which began as follows: "America is in peril. The welfare of American men and women and the future of our youth are at stake. . . . For three long years the New Deal administration has dishonored American traditions . . . The powers of Congress have been usurped by the president. . . . The rights and liberties of American citizens have been violated. Regulated monopoly has displaced free enterprise. The New Deal administration . . . has bred fear and hesitation in commerce and industry, thus discouraging new enterprises, preventing employment and prolonging the depression. . . . It has destroyed the morale of our people and made them dependent upon government. . . . To a free people, these actions are insufferable. . . . We invite all Americans, irrespective of party, to join us in defense of American institutions."

When they met in Cleveland on June 9, 1936, the Republicans nominated Kansas governor Alfred M. Landon for president of the United States. Their image-makers attempted to contrast Landon, the honest, hardworking man from the country's "farm belt," with Roosevelt, the overly sophisticated man born to privilege. The strategy was to try and win over enough of middle America to steal the election. They appealed to what they believed was a popular desire to return to simpler days, before the Depression and before Roosevelt's New Deal. They felt, and hoped the American people would agree, that Roosevelt had turned government into an enormous and costly bureaucratic monster. The Republicans shrewdly chose as their campaign theme the traditional folk song "Oh, Susannah" in order to lay further emphasis on Landon's homespun image.

On Election Day, Roosevelt carried all but two states, Maine and Vermont, in an overwhelming victory. He won reelection with 27.7 million votes, sixty percent of the total cast. The landslide represented a clear mandate from the American people. However, a major obstacle to the continuance of the New Deal era remained — the U.S. Supreme Court.

During his first term, Roosevelt had watched the Court declare several of his initiatives to be in violation of the separation of powers outlined in the Constitution. Among these were the National Industrial Recovery Act (NIRA) and the first Agricultural Adjustments Act. Under the system of checks and balances provided by the Constitution, the three branches of the Federal government — the executive, the legislative, and the judicial — must share power equally. When the Supreme Court finds that the executive or legislative branch exercises too much power, it may check the actions of that branch to

Eleanor Roosevelt was a particularly dynamic First Lady. In fact, in many respects she was Franklin's "eyes and ears," keeping him informed about people and places he could not personally visit because of his polio. Eleanor campaigned on behalf of a number of causes, among them the rights of women and organized labor and improvements in the school and welfare systems.

maintain the balance of power among the three. Roosevelt struggled with the Supreme Court because at the time its justices were staunch conservatives who disagreed with his political methods. Rather than accept the idea that the nation was doomed to four more years at the mercy of a conservative Supreme Court, Roosevelt resolved to reshape the court to make it more agreeable to New Deal legislation.

In February 1937, Roosevelt proposed that Congress consider a measure to restructure the Supreme Court. During Roosevelt's second term, there were nine justices sitting on the Supreme Court, as there had been since 1869. It was not unusual to change the number of Supreme Court justices. That had already been done six times in the nation's history. But the number of justices had been set at nine for more than half a century, so most people were suspicious of Roosevelt's motives. Roosevelt proposed that the chief executive be empowered to appoint an additional justice to the Court, but no more than six, whenever a sitting justice reached the age of seventy and chose not to retire within six months. Six Supreme Court justices were already seventy or older, and four of them were conservatives. This meant that Roosevelt would be able to "pack" the Court in his favor by appointing six pro-New Deal justices. Since the U.S. Constitution does not specify the number of justices to sit on the court, Roosevelt's proposal could not be considered unconstitutional.

While Congress considered the proposal, the Court reviewed and legally sanctioned two important pieces of New Deal legislation. These were the

Wagner Act and the Social Security Act. Also, a conservative Supreme Court justice, Willis Van Devanter, retired to his farm in Maryland, leaving Roosevelt the opportunity to appoint a liberal justice to the Court. This made the restructuring of the Court less important for the time being. Nevertheless Roosevelt had long-term New Deal goals in mind and wanted to be able to rely on the Court's support to achieve them. He pressed for Congress's approval.

But Roosevelt had failed to anticipate the opposition his proposal would encounter. Newspaper editorials accused the president of tampering with the court. The legal profession recommended rejection of the proposal. In Congress both Democrats and Republicans disapproved, enough so that a defeat of the bill seemed possible. The American people seemed divided on the issue. For many the Constitution, and the Supreme Court as its overseer, were part of the country's foundation and not to be meddled with. Others, in addition to being loyal to the president, felt the Supreme Court consisted of a bunch of stuffy old men who at best reflected the views of a previous generation and that, with several justices nearing eighty, the court should be kept vital with new blood.

On July 20, 1936, Roosevelt's Supreme Court bill went up in flames when the Senate voted it down by a margin of seventy to twenty. It was a bitter defeat for the president. Not only had he pushed hard for a doomed piece of legislation. He had also divided the members of his party, many of whom had forcefully opposed the bill.

Ironically, despite his failure to win approval for the

Supreme Court bill, Roosevelt was still able to re-make the Court to his liking. First, he filled the Van Devanter vacancy with a loyal New Dealer, Alabama Senator Hugo L. Black. Though it was revealed prior to his confirmation that Black was a former member of the Ku Klux Klan, a racist organization, he was confirmed by the Senate, sixty-three to thirteen. Then, in the next few years, seven other justices retired from the Supreme Court. Roosevelt promptly filled those vacancies with New Deal compatriots. The new Supreme Court justices were Stanley F. Reed, Felix Frankfurter, William O. Douglas, Frank Murphy, James F. Byrnes, Robert H. Jackson, and Wiley B. Rutledge. Once they had taken their places, seven out of the nine justices sitting on the Court were Roosevelt appointees.

Now Roosevelt had the Court he wanted. However, by splitting his own party in the fight for the Supreme Court bill, he had angered a good many senators and congressmen who had previously been his allies. He was eager to push further for social and economic reforms, but he now encountered resistance from the more conservative members of the legislature, Republicans and Democrats alike. Some believed the New Deal had gotten out of hand. They felt that there had to be a limit to the number of social programs created, and that that limit had been reached. They thought it best to pause for the time being and observe the results of the programs that had been put in place during Roosevelt's first term. Then it would be time to move forward. Others took a more extreme position. They believed that the

New Deal was, essentially, socialism in disguise. Though worth trying out of desperation in 1932, these people argued it was now leading America down the wrong path.

The results of Roosevelt's first term continued to receive mixed reviews. This unsteady support hindered his effectiveness during his second term. For example, some blamed the Wagner Act for the wave of violent labor strikes that was sweeping the country. At the same time, unemployment was now slowly rising again. This was happening even though, initially, unemployment had been reduced by the various New Deal social programs. In October 1937 prices on the New York Stock Exchange skidded. In November and December of that year more than one million people lost their jobs. Efforts to stem the rising unemployment rate were futile.

One segment of American society, the nation's black people, was ignored by Roosevelt's New Deal policies. Most blacks were tenant farmers, farm laborers, migrants, or domestic workers who worked outside the normal, official channels of employer and employee. Thus, most New Deal benefits such as unemployment insurance, minimum wages, and Social Security passed them by. Moreover, segregation, or separation, of blacks and whites was the rule that kept blacks in substandard housing and schools and out of well-paying jobs. Even the armed forces were segregated in the 1930s.

In the Harlem area of New York City, approximately 10,000 poor black families lived in rat-infested cellars. Medical treatment for blacks was

91

virtually nonexistent, and crime in America's black communities was rising steadily. Frustration erupted in violence in March 1935, when thousands of blacks rioted in the streets of Harlem, destroying property and shops owned by whites. It took 700 policemen to restore order. Despite the severity of the problems in the black communities, Roosevelt never addressed these issues. Some say he feared disturbing his relations with senators and other supporters in the South, where the use of blacks for cheap labor meant large profits for factory and farm owners.

Still, blacks felt for the most part that the New Deal policies were motivated by genuine compassion for the less fortunate. This gave them and other poor Americans hope because, at the very least, change was taking place, even if for now it was not affecting their lives in any dramatic way.

A significant number of important social programs, particularly those designed to support the labor movement, were enacted during Roosevelt's second term. For instance, the Fair Labor Standards Act was made law in June 1938. This provided for a minimum wage, regular salary increases over a seven-year period, a forty-hour work week, and the abolition of child labor in all industries that dealt in interstate commerce. Also, as a result of the Wagner Act, Roosevelt's second term saw the formation of many large and small labor unions. In November of that year, for example, the Congress of Industrial Organizations (CIO) met in Pittsburgh to hold its first convention. The CIO was a federation of unions counting as its members nearly four million workers from the steel, coal-mining, auto, electrical, and other industries. Like the American Federation of Labor (AFL), established in 1886, the CIO would act as a powerful force for the rights of workers for years to come.

Many of the labor policies Roosevelt instituted during his first two terms have endured to this day. For example, since the Roosevelt era, employers have been required to pay workers no less than the minimum wage prescribed by the federal government. Though today many Americans earning the minimum wage live below the poverty level, the existence of a set minimum wage continues to prevent at least some greedy employers from engaging in unfair labor practices by paying laborers wages so low they can't afford food and shelter.

The worker in American society enjoys other benefits today that are also fruits of Roosevelt's New Deal. These include workers' compensation, disability insurance, a forty-hour work week, vacations and sick time with pay, Social Security payments in old age, retirement pensions, and the abolition of child labor.

President Roosevelt might have been able to continue with the sweeping social reforms of the New Deal if he had not been forced, a little more than halfway through his second term to turn his attention to foreign affairs. But the domestic problems that had been so pressing were suddenly overshadowed by a larger threat looming on the horizon: Europe was at war.

8

World at War

The bitter memories of World War I remained vivid through the 1920s and 1930s. In fact, in the decades following the war the United States followed an isolationist foreign policy, which meant that it preferred not to get involved with world affairs in the form of wars, alliances, treaties, and the like. Most Americans felt that if war again broke out in Europe it would be best for the United States to remain neutral, to secure its own borders and not get involved in the business of other nations. America's isolationist position took the form of a total arms embargo when Congress passed the Neutrality Act in 1935 and another neutrality bill in 1937, both prohibiting the shipment of U.S. arms abroad.

In a 1936 address, Roosevelt detailed U.S. foreign policy at the time: "As a consistent part of a clear policy, the United States is following a twofold neutrality toward any and all nations that engage in wars that are not of immediate concern to the Americas. First, we decline to encourage the prosecution of war by permitting belligerents to obtain arms . . . from the United States. Second, we seek to discourage the use by belligerent nations of any and all American products calculated to facilitate the prosecution of a war in quantities over and above our normal exports of them in time of peace."

During the late 1930s, America's isolationism had grave consequences abroad. Spain was torn by a civil war in which a Republican government was threatened by the forces of fascist dictator Francisco Franco. Fascism is a philosophy of government based on the belief that power should be exercised by a dictator and that any opposition and criticism should be suppressed by force. Spanish freedom fighters were losing a bloody struggle and asked the United States to help their cause by sending weapons and supplies. The American people were mixed in their feelings about American neutrality. Most dreaded the prospect of involvement in another war. But others were so sympathetic with the Republicans' cause that they went to Spain themselves to bear arms against the fascists. The Roosevelt administration remained uninvolved in the Spanish Civil War, preferring isolationism to an engaged struggle for liberty abroad. After much bloodshed, Franco's troops overthrew the Republican government.

Roosevelt asked Congress to repeal the arms embargo in 1935, when Italy invaded the African country of Ethiopia. But the isolationist sentiment in Congress could not be shaken. When the Germans invaded Poland in 1939, and France and Great Britain, Poland's allies, declared war on Germany, Roosevelt called a special session of Congress. He pleaded with the legislators to allow him to send arms to Europe to quell the advance of the Germans. This time Congress reconsidered. In November 1939 a "cash-and-carry" policy went into effect. This allowed France and England to buy military equipment from the United States as long as they paid cash and carried the supplies away on their own ships.

The German advance was orchestrated by Adolf Hitler. Hitler was a brutal dictator and a fanatical nationalist. He became German chancellor in 1933 during a time when Germany, in the aftermath of World War I and the Treaty of Versailles, was desperate for leadership. He proclaimed what he believed was the superiority of the white, Nordic, or Aryan race over all other peoples, particularly the Jews. He and the Nazi Party blamed the Jewish people for the country's social and economic ills since World War I. He eventually sought to destroy them through the implementation of a murderous program called the Final Solution. He envisioned a world dominated by the Aryan race, and he pursued that end ruthlessly through military might abroad and police power at home. His philosophy of hatred and aggression stood in stark contrast to Roosevelt's sincere compassion.

Hitler's successes were frightening for Roosevelt and the free world to witness. In the spring of 1940, Germany moved into Denmark, Norway, Holland, Luxembourg, and Belgium. On June 10, Italy joined

97

forces with Germany and attacked France. After only twelve days, France surrendered. In September the Germans began to bomb London from the air. Shocked by these developments, Roosevelt stepped up U.S. military aid to the besieged "Allies," and Congress passed the first peacetime military draft in U.S. history.

Most Americans believed the United States had to stay out of the war in Europe. Still, the country's isolationist foreign policy ended with the prospect of Europe falling to fascism. The Hitler menace was so extreme that eventually few Americans questioned the need for the United States to become involved in the conflict.

The year the Germans occupied Paris, 1940, was an election year in the United States. Roosevelt decided to seek a third term as the nation's president. His decision was unprecedented. No U.S. president had ever served more than two terms. Roosevelt had planned to retire to Hyde Park to spend the rest of his life comfortably without the burdens of public office. He had been looking forward to writing his memoirs and to being in the peaceful surroundings of his childhood home in the Hudson Valley. However, with the Nazis trampling through Europe, Roosevelt contemplated the prospect of a third term:

"I have asked myself whether I have the right, as commander-in-chief of the army and navy, to call men and women to serve their country or to train themselves to serve, and, at the same time decline to serve my country in my own personal capacity, if I am called upon to do so by the people of my country. . . . Today, all private plans, all private lives, have been in a sense repealed by an overriding public danger. In the face of that public danger all those who can be of service to the Republic have no choice but to offer themselves for service in those capacities for which they may be fitted. . . . I had made plans for myself, plans for a private life . . . but my conscience will not let me turn my back on a call to service."

The Republicans met in Philadelphia in June to nominate their candidate. After considering several, including the son of former President William Howard Taft, they selected Indiana businessman and Wall Street lawyer Wendell L. Willkie. A moderate conservative — and at one time a registered Democrat — Willkie had supported New Deal legislation and the labor movement. Still, in an article in the April 1940 issue of *Fortune* magazine he strongly criticized Roosevelt's social-welfare policies. He also warned the voters of the dangers of allowing one man to serve as president for twelve years.

Given Roosevelt's worsening paralysis, many Americans had doubts about Roosevelt's ability to serve. It was also clear that his first two terms had taken a serious toll on his general health. He had aged noticeably. There were large, dark circles around his eyes. Both his face and upper body drooped as if the years in office had made him weary. Roosevelt's mind, however, was as sharp as ever, and everyone who saw him in public or heard him on the radio knew he was still the person for the job.

On July 17, the Democrats unanimously nomi-

President Roosevelt flanked by Prime Minister Winston
Churchill of Great Britain (left) and Premier Josef Stalin of the
Soviet Union in Yalta, in the southwestern Soviet Union,
February 1945. With an Allied victory in World War II close at
hand, the leaders of the "big three" powers were meeting to
discuss post-war military and political arrangements.

nated President Roosevelt to run for a third term. Busy with the affairs of state, he did not begin active- ly campaigning until October 23, when he gave the first of five lengthy campaign speeches. Roosevelt spoke proudly of the achievements of his first two terms, criticized the Republicans for stretching the truth and making empty promises in their cam- paign, and called for national unity. He restated with conviction his position that the United States would not fight in a foreign war unless attacked. He closed his speeches with the words, "It is for peace that I have labored; and it is for peace that I shall labor all the days of my life."

Just as they had four years before, more Ameri- cans voted for their president than for his Republican opponent. Roosevelt won the election handily, receiv- ing 27,243,466 votes to Willkie's 22,304,755. The final tally of electoral votes was 449 for the Demo- crats and eighty-two for the Republicans.

By December 1940, seriously drained of financial resources by the war, the British found themselves unable to pay cash to the United States for war sup- plies. Roosevelt persuaded Congress to support a measure whereby the United States could lease mili- tary equipment to Great Britain on credit. The Lend Lease Act, as the measure was called, was passed by Congress in March 1941. Military aid to Great Britain was increased in an effort to stop Germany's con- quest of Europe.

In the meantime, Japan had allied itself with Ger- many and Italy to form the "Axis" powers. Japan was using military force to expand its influence in the

East, particularly in China, French Indochina, Singapore, and the Dutch East Indies. Roosevelt made an attempt to negotiate with the Japanese, but as the negotiations were still in process, Japan launched the devastating air attack on the U.S. naval base at Pearl Harbor, Hawaii, on December 7, 1941. Congress immediately issued a declaration of war against Japan. On December 11, Germany and Italy declared war on the United States.

Two weeks after the attack on Pearl Harbor, Roosevelt met with British Prime Minister Winston Churchill in Washington, D.C., to forge an alliance and to coordinate the military effort. Suddenly Roosevelt was more than America's New Deal President. By virtue of the enormous size, incredible wealth, and great military strength of the United States, President Roosevelt was also the leader of the free world.

Though a number of pressing domestic problems continued to demand his attention, Roosevelt was forced to devote the bulk of his energy to winning the war. He visited factories and military installations, inspiring those directly involved in the war effort to display courage in facing its challenges. He continued to hold regular press conferences to keep the American people informed. He frequently took to the airwaves for fireside chats in which he offered detailed progress reports about the conflict as millions of concerned Americans listened intently. Clearly, Roosevelt was the same great leader the nation had witnessed during his first hundred days. But now he had become a figure of global significance, and he rose to the challenge. Roosevelt and Churchill would work closely throughout the war in a concerted effort to rid the world of the Nazi threat.

The attack on Pearl Harbor had also aroused the American people, who bravely took on the challenge of the war effort. American servicemen were sent to fight in Europe, Africa, and Asia. American civilians did everything they could in the name of patriotism and the defeat of the Nazis. Many of the nation's factories and other production facilities were given over to creation of materials that would be used for the war. This meant that goods such as meat, coffee, sugar, gasoline, and cigarettes had to be rationed. Still, Americans were united in a single purpose, and the country's morale remained high.

The war also revitalized the U.S. economy, bringing the Depression to an end once and for all. As the need for labor increased with America's involvement in the war, the unemployment rate in the United States dropped steadily. Workers in American factories and shipyards worked around the clock manufacturing airplanes, tanks, ships, weapons, ammunition, and other supplies. The nation was determined to emerge victorious, and its healthier economy provided a feeling of power.

Still, the Allies continued to struggle in 1942. Though American forces made headway against the Japanese in the Central Pacific that spring, by July the Japanese had seized several of the Aleutian Islands, off the coast of Alaska. In Europe, Hitler's forces moved further into the Soviet Union, taking control of major Russian cities along the way. The bloodshed continued in all corners of the world with no apparent end in sight.

Then the momentum slowly changed in favor of the Allies. That summer, in the South Pacific, American forces emerged victorious in a long battle against the Japanese at Guadalcanal, in the Solomon Islands. The British, who had suffered devastating losses fighting in Africa, defeated the Germans in the Battle of El Alamein in Egypt in October and suddenly were turning back German attacks on all fronts. The Soviet Union, also one of the Allied powers, was also successful against the Germans, particularly north of Moscow and in the Caucasus region in southwestern Russia. Then, following several crucial defeats in Africa, Italian dictator Benito Mussolini resigned. It was becoming clear that a last, all-out offensive could bring about an end to the war and, ultimately, victory for the Allies.

Roosevelt met frequently with the other Allied heads of state — Churchill and Joseph Stalin, leader of the Soviet Union — as the war in Europe continued. In 1943, Roosevelt met with Churchill in Casablanca, Morocco. There they agreed that Germany, Japan, and Italy would have to surrender unconditionally. They believed that nothing less than complete surrender by the Axis powers would ensure the security of the free world. They disagreed as to when to launch a major offensive against the German barricades on the shores of Normandy, France. Stalin and various U.S. generals urged the earliest date possible. Churchill argued for a "soft underbelly" approach through Italy first. Finally, the British Prime

Minister was able to persuade Roosevelt to delay the offensive, which at the time was scheduled for August, until the following year.

When he returned to Washington, Roosevelt played host to several dignitaries, including the wife of Chinese nationalist Chiang Kai-shek. Churchill visited Hyde Park in August 1943, and later that year the two met again in Cairo, Egypt, to discuss the problems in the East. The "Big Three" — as Roosevelt, Churchill, and Stalin were called — met together for the first time in Teheran, Iran, in November 1943. There they discussed the plans for the Normandy landing and considered the post-war fate of Germany and the Eastern European countries Hitler had conquered during the war. From there, Roosevelt continued his diplomatic tour of duty, flying back to Cairo and then to Tunis, Sicily, and Malta. By the time he returned to Washington, he had spent more than two months abroad.

The Allied forces moved into North Africa and Italy and continued to make great strides in the war with Japan. On June 6, 1944, Allied forces directed by General Dwight D. Eisenhower landed on the coast of Normandy, France. This massive strike and battle was known as D-day. (The military often uses the letter "D" to designate a day for launching an operation.) D-day was the first in a series of Allied victories that led to the liberation of Paris on August 25. It was the most crucial step toward achieving an overall victory in Europe.

In 1944, Roosevelt was faced once again with the decision of whether to seek another term as president.

He was now sixty-two years old and had not known the best of health during his third term. U.S. presidents usually seem to age quickly while in office. It was no surprise that Roosevelt, having served three terms during an extremely difficult period in American history, looked tired. Still, Roosevelt felt he had to see the war to its conclusion. He could not imagine stepping down before the job was done.

New York Governor Thomas E. Dewey accepted the Republican nomination for president on June 28, 1944, in Chicago. Dewey described the Roosevelt administration as "exhausted, quarreling, and bickering." He criticized the Democrats for high taxes and continued labor unrest at home, and he made the President's failing health an important campaign issue. Indeed, Roosevelt himself had doubts about his health and whether he was up to the task of four more years in the White House. Was Roosevelt too old and tired to lead the nation to peace? The American voters did not think so. On November 7, 1944, Roosevelt was reelected by a 3.6 million popular-vote margin. He also dominated the electoral college, receiving 432 electoral votes to Dewey's ninety-nine.

In February 1945, the Big Three met in the Soviet Union in the city of Yalta, located in an area known as the Crimea. There they made the final preparations for Germany's defeat. They planned a coordinated attack on Germany and further discussed the treatment of those countries that would be liberated after Germany's surrender. Also at the Yalta conference, the Russians agreed to enter the fight against the Japanese to hasten an Allied victory in the East. Stalin was also persuaded to attend a conference in the United States, to take part in a plan to create a world peace organization. The organization eventually established is known today as the United Nations.

On March 7, 1945, the Allies launched a "final" offensive in the vicinity of Remagen, Germany, on the east bank of the Rhine River. It soon became clear that an Allied victory was soon to be had. Roosevelt, however, did not live to see Germany defeated. On April 12, 1945, while resting at Warm Springs, he suffered a massive cerebral hemorrhage and died. He was sixty-three years old. For more than thirty years he had exerted his life's energy in the service of his country. Eleanor, who was in Washington that spring, received word of her husband's death by telephone. She flew to Warm Springs at once to bring her husband's body home. On May 7, the Germans surrendered. The war in Europe, and an era in American political history as well, were over.

9

The Roosevelt Legacy

In his time, Franklin Roosevelt was an extremely controversial public figure. He was hated by a good many Americans and loved by many others. He accepted his country's highest office during perhaps the lowest period in its history, the Great Depression, and took drastic measures to revitalize the American economy. He put America back to work, and his optimism and charm restored the country's confidence. When he contracted the polio virus in the prime of his life, he struggled with intense pain. Still, he always managed a smile and never surrendered in his battle with the crippling disease. Then, when the United States became embroiled in World War II, Roosevelt's unique brand of courage and determination inspired the American people to work together and give their all to stop fascism in its tracks.

Today, as in Franklin Roosevelt's time, American political debate often focuses on the issue of the proper function of government. Should government be large or small? Should government stay out of the affairs of big business and trust that profits will trickle down to the workers, as Hoover and the conservatives believed it should? Or is it necessary for government to regulate business and for workers to unionize in order to safeguard society against greed and exploitation? Should government provide assistance for the needy in the form of basic housing and health care? Not every American during Roosevelt's era agreed with the answers he proposed to these questions. But he took action with conviction, and many were grateful for his having done so. Many Americans today admire the man for his tremendous contribution to the improvement of American society and to communicating the importance of democracy around the world. Even conservatives whose political beliefs are contrary to those of Roosevelt recognize his many great accomplishments.

The life of Franklin Roosevelt has been examined, discussed, and written about perhaps more than any U.S. president. But, perhaps because he kept no diary, there continues to be a mystique surrounding his life. Numerous books and articles have been written on the subject of his private life, and people from coast to coast and abroad travel many miles to visit the Roosevelt house in Hyde Park and the summer cottage on Campobello Island to gaze at Roosevelt memorabilia preserved in glass cases. Some visit the Roosevelt homes simply for an illustrative lesson in history. Others are driven by a desire to get a glimpse into the life and times of one of the greatest men of our century.

Franklin Delano Roosevelt, the thirty-second president of the United States, inspired a generation with his adept leadership. He comforted his people in a time of domestic trouble, led his nation to victory in history's most devastating war, gave hope to people everywhere as leader of the free world, and overcame seemingly insurmountable obstacles, including intense physical pain, to do so. Most historians agree that he acted with unprecedented intelligence and daring to save his nation's economy during the toughest of times and to help rid the world of the threat of dictatorship.

Other books you might enjoy reading

1. Alsop, Joseph. *FDR: A Centenary Remembrance.* Viking Press, 1982.

2. Burns, James MacGregor. *Roosevelt: The Lion and the Fox.* Harcourt, Brace, Jovanovich, 1963.

3. Davis, Kenneth S. *FDR: The Beckoning of Destiny.* G.P. Putnam's Sons, 1972.

4. Gallagher, Hugh G. *FDR's Splendid Deception.* Dodd, Mead & Company, 1985.

5. Lash, Joseph. *Eleanor and Franklin.* New American Library, 1973.

6. Leuchtenburg, William. *Franklin D. Roosevelt and the New Deal.* Harper & Row, 1963.

7. Roosevelt, Eleanor. *This I Remember.* Harper & Row, 1949.

8. Roosevelt, Eleanor. *This Is My Story.* Garden City Publishing Company, 1939.

ABOUT THE AUTHOR

John W. Selfridge is an editor and free-lance writer with a special interest in twentieth-century history and culture. He received an M.A. in 1980 from Columbia University, where he studied literature and philosophy, and he is currently enrolled at Rutgers University Law School. An editor for a major New York City publishing house, he has been consulted on more than 100 young adult biographies. He is the author of *John F. Kennedy: Courage in Crisis* in the Great Lives Series.